First World War
and Army of Occupation
War Diary
France, Belgium and Germany

59 DIVISION
176 Infantry Brigade
Prince of Wales's (North Staffordshire Regiment)
2/6th Battalion
2 February 1917 - 31 July 1918

WO95/3021/5

The Naval & Military Press Ltd
www.nmarchive.com
Published in association with The National Archives

Published by

The Naval & Military Press Ltd

Unit 10 Ridgewood Industrial Park,

Uckfield, East Sussex,

TN22 5QE England

Tel: +44 (0) 1825 749494

www.naval-military-press.com

www.nmarchive.com

This diary has been reprinted in facsimile from the original. Any imperfections are inevitably reproduced and the quality may fall short of modern type and cartographic standards.

© **Crown Copyright**
Images reproduced by permission of The National Archives, London, England, 2015.

Contents

Document type	Place/Title	Date From	Date To
Heading	WO95/3021/5		
Heading	59th Division 176th Infy Bde 2-6th Bn Nth Staffs Regt 1917 Feb-1918 Jly		
Heading	War Diary of 2/6th Bn North Stafford Rgt From 2nd Feby 1917 To 28th February 1917 Volume III		
War Diary	Codford	02/02/1917	23/02/1917
War Diary	Southampton	23/02/1917	23/02/1917
War Diary	Codford	24/02/1917	24/02/1917
War Diary	Le Havre	24/02/1917	25/02/1917
War Diary	Folkestone	25/02/1917	25/02/1917
War Diary	Boulogne	25/02/1917	26/02/1917
War Diary	Saleux	26/02/1917	26/02/1917
War Diary	Boulogne	27/02/1917	27/02/1917
War Diary	Saleux	27/02/1917	27/02/1917
War Diary	Longeaux	27/02/1917	27/02/1917
War Diary	Fouilloy	27/02/1917	28/02/1917
War Diary	Morcourt	28/02/1917	28/02/1917
Heading	War Diary of 2/6th Bn North Staffs Regt From 1st March 1917 To 29th March 1917 Volume III		
War Diary	Morcourt	01/03/1917	06/03/1917
War Diary	Foucaucourt	07/03/1917	07/03/1917
War Diary	Trenches	08/03/1917	11/03/1917
War Diary	Berny	11/03/1917	15/03/1917
War Diary	Foucaucourt	15/03/1917	15/03/1917
War Diary	Trenches	17/03/1917	17/03/1917
War Diary	Mazincourt	18/03/1917	21/03/1917
War Diary	Misery	21/03/1917	28/03/1917
War Diary	Estrees-En-Chausses	28/03/1917	29/03/1917
Heading	2/6th North Staffs Regt War Diary From 1st April 1917 To 30th April 1917 Volume 3 Pages 5 To 8		
War Diary	Boucly	01/04/1917	08/04/1917
War Diary	Hervilly	09/04/1917	10/04/1917
War Diary	Jeancourt	10/04/1917	15/04/1917
War Diary	L.28.a.5.4 (Sheet 62cNE)	16/04/1917	17/04/1917
War Diary	Jeancourt	17/04/1917	28/04/1917
War Diary	Bernes	29/04/1917	30/04/1917
Heading	War Diary of 2/6th North Stafford Regiment From 1st May 1917 To 31st May 1917 Vol 4		
War Diary	Bernes	01/05/1917	01/05/1917
War Diary	Nobescourt Farm	02/05/1917	06/05/1917
War Diary	L.10.a.6.4	06/05/1917	10/05/1917
War Diary	Roisel	11/05/1917	12/05/1917
War Diary	L.10.a.6.4	14/05/1917	19/05/1917
War Diary	Roisel	20/05/1917	20/05/1917
War Diary	Villers Faucon	23/05/1917	31/05/1917
War Diary	Equancourt	31/05/1917	31/05/1917
Heading	War Diary of 2/6th North Stafford Regiment From 1st June 1917 To 30th June 1917 Vol 5		
War Diary	Eqvancourt	01/06/1917	11/06/1917
War Diary	Q.10.d.4.8	12/06/1917	22/06/1917

War Diary	P.2.6.9.1	23/06/1917	29/06/1917
Heading	War Diary of 2/6th North Stafford Regiment From 1st July 1917 To 31st July 1917 Vol 6		
War Diary	V.16.b.1.2	01/07/1917	07/07/1917
War Diary	O.10.c.3.5	08/07/1917	27/07/1917
Heading	War Diary of 2/6th Bn North Staffordshire Regiment From 1st Aug 1917 To 31st Aug 1917 Vol 7		
War Diary	Haplincourt	06/08/1917	23/08/1917
War Diary	Forceville	24/08/1917	31/08/1917
Heading	War Diary of 2/6th Bn North Stafford Regiment From 1st Sept 1917 To 30th Sept 1917 Vol 8		
War Diary	Winnezeele	01/09/1917	30/09/1917
Heading	War Diary of 2/6th Bn North Staffs Regiment From 1st Oct 1917 To 31st Oct 1917 Vol 9		
War Diary	Isbergues	01/10/1917	04/10/1917
War Diary	Predefin	07/10/1917	12/10/1917
War Diary	Lievin	13/10/1917	28/10/1917
War Diary	Souchez	29/10/1917	31/10/1917
Heading	War Diary of 2/6th North Staffs Regiment From 1st Nov 1917 To 30th Nov 1917		
War Diary	Souchez	01/11/1917	12/11/1917
War Diary	Avion	13/11/1917	14/11/1917
War Diary	Souchez	17/11/1917	19/11/1917
War Diary	Simencourt	20/11/1917	21/11/1917
War Diary	Achiet	22/11/1917	22/11/1917
War Diary	Heudicourt	23/11/1917	27/11/1917
War Diary	Cambrai Front	28/11/1917	30/11/1917
Heading	War Diary of 2/6th North Staffs Regiment From 1st Dec 1917 To 31st Dec 1917 Vol 11		
War Diary	Bourlon Wood	01/12/1917	01/12/1917
War Diary	Flesquieres	02/12/1917	04/12/1917
War Diary	Lechelle	05/12/1917	08/12/1917
War Diary	Rue	10/12/1917	31/12/1917
Heading	War Diary of 2/6th Bn North Staffs Regiment From 1st Jan 1918 To 31st Jan 1918 Vol 12		
War Diary	Rue	06/01/1918	22/01/1918
War Diary	Rebreuviette	23/01/1918	31/01/1918
Heading	War Diary of 2/6th North Staffs Regiment From 1st Feb 1918 To 28th Feb 1918 Vol 13		
War Diary	Rebreuviette	05/02/1918	09/02/1918
War Diary	Noreuil	10/02/1918	28/02/1918
Heading	59th Division 176th Infantry Brigade War Diary 2/6th Battalion North Staffordshire Regiment March 1918		
Heading	War Diary of 2/6th Bn North Staffs Regiment From 1st March 1918 To 31st March 1918 Vol 14		
War Diary	Noreuil Mory	01/03/1918	13/03/1918
War Diary	Bullecourt	19/03/1918	21/03/1918
War Diary	Courcelles Les Comte	21/03/1918	21/03/1918
War Diary	Douchy	22/03/1918	23/03/1918
War Diary	Bouzincourt	25/03/1918	25/03/1918
War Diary	Beaucourt	26/03/1918	26/03/1918
War Diary	Fienvillers-Candas	26/03/1918	28/03/1918
War Diary	La Pougnay	29/03/1918	29/03/1918
War Diary	Caucourt	30/03/1918	30/03/1918
Map	Ecoust (Neighbourhood) From Memory		

Type	Description	Date From	Date To
Miscellaneous	21st March 1918 An Account Of Events As Regards 2/6th North Staffordshire Regt (Battn Headquarters And A & B Coys) On That Date	21/03/1918	21/03/1918
Heading	176th Brigade 59th Division 2/6th Battalion North Staffordshire Regiment April 1918		
Heading	War Diary of 2/6th Bn North Staffs Regiment From 1st April 1918 To 30th April 1918		
War Diary	Caucourt	01/04/1918	01/04/1918
War Diary	Proven	01/04/1918	01/04/1918
War Diary	St Jans-Der-Biezen	02/04/1918	06/04/1918
War Diary	Trappistes Farm	10/04/1918	10/04/1918
War Diary	Ypres	11/04/1918	13/04/1918
War Diary	Brandhoek	13/04/1918	13/04/1918
War Diary	Reninghelst	14/04/1918	14/04/1918
War Diary	Locre	15/04/1918	15/04/1918
War Diary	Bailleul	15/04/1918	15/04/1918
War Diary	Locre	16/04/1918	18/04/1918
War Diary	Terdinghem	19/04/1918	19/04/1918
War Diary	Peselhoek	21/04/1918	24/04/1918
War Diary	Ellink	26/04/1918	27/04/1918
Heading	2/6th N. Staffs Regt War Diary For Month Of May 1918 Volume III		
War Diary	Ouderdom Switch Line	01/05/1918	05/05/1918
War Diary	Trappist Farm	06/05/1918	06/05/1918
War Diary	Kinderbeck	07/05/1918	10/05/1918
War Diary	Mametz	11/05/1918	11/05/1918
War Diary	Fiefs	14/05/1918	14/05/1918
War Diary	Magnicourt-En-Comte	15/05/1918	15/05/1918
War Diary	Fiefs	15/05/1918	15/05/1918
War Diary	Habacq	16/05/1918	16/05/1918
War Diary	Lattre St-Quentin	17/05/1918	19/05/1918
War Diary	Magnicourt-En-Comte	20/05/1918	20/05/1918
War Diary	Livossart	21/05/1918	21/05/1918
War Diary	Inghem	24/05/1918	28/05/1918
War Diary	Pont De Briques	29/05/1918	29/05/1918
War Diary	Canchy	29/05/1918	31/05/1918
Operation(al) Order(s)	Operation Order No.21 A By Lieut. Colonel J.H. Porter, D.S.O. Cmdg 2/6th North Staffordshire Regiment.	05/05/1918	05/05/1918
Operation(al) Order(s)	Operation Order No.22 A By Lieut. Colonel J.H. Porter, D.S.O. Cmdg 2/6th North Staffordshire Regiment.		
Operation(al) Order(s)	Operation Order No.30 By Lieut. Colonel J.H. Porter, D.S.O. Cmdg 2/6th North Staffordshire Regiment.	08/05/1918	08/05/1918
Operation(al) Order(s)	Operation Order No.31 By Lieut. Colonel J.H. Porter, D.S.O. Cmdg 2/6th North Staffordshire Regiment.	09/05/1918	09/05/1918
Operation(al) Order(s)	Operation Order No.32 By Lieut. Colonel J.H. Porter, D.S.O. Cmdg 2/6th North Staffordshire Regiment.	10/05/1918	10/05/1918
Operation(al) Order(s)	Operation Order No.34 By Lieut. Colonel J.H. Porter, D.S.O. Cmdg 2/6th North Staffordshire Regiment.	14/05/1918	14/05/1918
Operation(al) Order(s)	Operation Order No.35 By Lieut. Colonel J.H. Porter, D.S.O. Cmdg 2/6th North Staffordshire Regiment.	19/05/1918	19/05/1918
Operation(al) Order(s)	Operation Order No.35a By Lieut. Colonel J.H. Porter, D.S.O. Cmdg 2/6th North Staffordshire Regiment.	15/05/1918	15/05/1918
Operation(al) Order(s)	Operation Order No.36 By Lieut. Colonel J.H. Porter, D.S.O. Cmdg 2/6th North Staffordshire Regiment.	18/05/1918	18/05/1918

Type	Description	Start	End
Operation(al) Order(s)	Operation Order No.37 By Lieut. Colonel J.H. Porter, D.S.O. Cmdg 2/6th North Staffordshire Regiment.	19/05/1918	19/05/1918
Operation(al) Order(s)	Operation Order No.38 By Lieut. Colonel J.H. Porter, D.S.O. Cmdg 2/6th North Staffordshire Regiment.	20/05/1918	20/05/1918
Operation(al) Order(s)	Operation Order No.39 By Lieut. Colonel J.H. Porter, D.S.O. Cmdg 2/6th North Staffordshire Regiment.	27/05/1918	27/05/1918
Heading	66th Division 2-6th Bn Nth Staffs Regt. Jun 1918 & July		
Heading	2/6th N. Staffs Regt War Diary For Month Of June 1918 Volume III		
War Diary	Canchy	01/06/1918	07/06/1918
War Diary	Montieres	08/06/1918	17/06/1918
War Diary	Miannay	19/06/1918	19/06/1918
War Diary	Bazinval	20/06/1918	21/06/1918
War Diary	Pierregot	21/06/1918	21/06/1918
War Diary	Molliens Au Bois	23/06/1918	26/06/1918
War Diary	Pierregot	27/06/1918	27/06/1918
War Diary	St Ouen	28/06/1918	28/06/1918
War Diary	Yaucourt-Bussus	30/06/1918	30/06/1918
War Diary	Canchy	01/06/1918	07/06/1918
War Diary	Montieres	08/06/1918	17/06/1918
War Diary	Miannay	19/06/1918	19/06/1918
War Diary	Bazinval	20/06/1918	21/06/1918
War Diary	Pierregot	21/06/1918	21/06/1918
War Diary	Molliens Au Bois	23/06/1918	26/06/1918
War Diary	Pierregot	27/06/1918	27/06/1918
War Diary	St. Ouen	28/06/1918	28/06/1918
War Diary	Yaucourt-Bussus	30/06/1918	30/06/1918
Heading	2/6th North Staffs Regt War Diary For Month Of July 1918 Volume III		
Heading	2/6th North Staffs Regt War Diary For Month Of July 1918		
War Diary	Yaucourt-Bussus	01/07/1918	03/07/1918
War Diary	Bernaville	04/07/1918	04/07/1918
War Diary	Doullens	06/07/1918	22/07/1918
War Diary	Serquex	23/07/1918	23/07/1918
War Diary	Abancourt Area	31/07/1918	31/07/1918
War Diary	Yaucourt-Bussus	01/07/1918	03/07/1918
War Diary	Bernaville	04/07/1918	04/07/1918
War Diary	Doullens	06/07/1918	22/07/1918
War Diary	Serquex	23/07/1918	23/07/1918
War Diary	Abancourt Area	31/07/1918	31/07/1918
Operation(al) Order(s)	Operation Order No. 40 By Lieut. Colonel J.H. Porter, D.S.O. Cmdg 2/6th North Staffordshire Regiment.	07/06/1918	07/06/1918
Operation(al) Order(s)	Operation Order No.40a By Lieut. Colonel J.H. Porter, D.S.O. Cmdg 2/6th North Staffordshire Regiment.	07/06/1918	07/06/1918
Operation(al) Order(s)	Operation Order No.41 By Lieut. Colonel J.H. Porter, D.S.O. Cmdg 2/6th North Staffordshire Regiment.	16/06/1918	16/06/1918
Operation(al) Order(s)	Operation Order No.42 By Lieut. Colonel J.H. Porter, D.S.O. Cmdg 2/6th North Staffordshire Regiment.	19/06/1918	19/06/1918
Operation(al) Order(s)	Operation Order No.43 By Lieut. Colonel J.H. Porter, D.S.O. Cmdg 2/6th North Staffordshire Regiment.	29/06/1918	29/06/1918
Operation(al) Order(s)	Operation Order No.44 By Lieut. Colonel J.H. Porter, D.S.O. Cmdg 2/6th North Staffordshire Regiment.	21/06/1918	21/06/1918
Operation(al) Order(s)	Operation Order No.45 By Lieut. Colonel J.H. Porter, D.S.O. Cmdg 2/6th North Staffordshire Regiment.	25/06/1918	25/06/1918

Operation(al) Order(s)	Operation Order No.46 By Lieut. Colonel J.H. Porter, D.S.O. Cmdg 2/6th North Staffordshire Regiment.	26/06/1918	26/06/1918
Operation(al) Order(s)	Operation Order No.47 By Lieut. Colonel J.H. Porter, D.S.O. Cmdg 2/6th North Staffordshire Regiment.	27/06/1918	27/06/1918
Operation(al) Order(s)	Operation Order No.48 By Lieut. Colonel J.H. Porter, D.S.O. Cmdg 2/6th North Staffordshire Regiment.	02/07/1918	02/07/1918
Operation(al) Order(s)	Operation Order No.49 By Lieut. Colonel J.H. Porter, D.S.O. Cmdg 2/6th North Staffordshire Regiment.	06/06/1918	06/06/1918
Operation(al) Order(s)	Operation Order No.50 By Lieut. Colonel J.H. Porter, D.S.O. Cmdg 2/6th North Staffordshire Regiment.	21/07/1918	21/07/1918
Miscellaneous	Operation Order No.50 By Lieut. Colonel J.H. Porter, D.S.O. Cmdg 2/6th North Staffordshire Regiment.	30/07/1918	30/07/1918
Miscellaneous	Routine Orders By Lieut Col. J.H.Porter, D.S.O. Cmdg 2/6th North Staffordshire Regiment	30/07/1918	30/07/1918

woos/300u/5

59TH DIVISION
176TH INFY BDE

2-6TH BN NTH STAFFS REGT.
~~FEB 1917-MAY 1918.~~
1917 FEB — 1918 JLY

DISBANDED 1918 JLY

Also 1916 JAN and FEB

Army Form C. 2118.

WAR DIARY
or
INTELLIGENCE SUMMARY
(Erase heading not required.)

Vol I

Confidential

WAR DIARY
of
2/6th Bn. North Stafford Rgt.

From:- 2nd Feby 1917. to:- 28th February 1917.

VOLUME III

Army Form C. 2118.

WAR DIARY
or
INTELLIGENCE SUMMARY
(Erase heading not required)

2/6TH BN. NORTH STAFFORD REGT.

VOLUME 3
Page 1.

Place	Date	Hour	Summary of Events and Information	Remarks and references to Appendices
CODFORD	2/2/17	24 oc	An Advance Party composed of 5 OR's 14 OR proceeds for instructional tour Overseas.	
Do.	23/2/17		CAPT. & ADJ. R.S. TENNENT admitted to Hospital.	
Do.	"	7.30 oc	BN 1ST LINE TRANSPORT with personnel and various details (64 H. 3 OR's. 89 OR inclusive 5 ASC cmg²) entrains for Overseas.	
SOUTHAMPTON	"	18 oc	BN 1ST LINE TRANSPORT &c embark for LE HAVRE (Troopship "SOUTH WESTERN MILLER")	
CODFORD	24/2/17		CAPT A.L. BODLEY (M.O.) admitted to Hospital.	
Do	"	23.35	BN (in two portions entrains	
LE HAVRE	"	8 oc	BN 1ST LINE TRANSPORT &c arrives.	
Do	"	17 oc	do. proceeds to Rest Camp	
Do	25/2/17	11 oc	do. entrains for LONGEAUX (where they are joined up by A & D Coys)	
FOLKESTONE	"	7 oc	BN arrives FOLKESTONE	
Do	"	10 oc	BN embarks for BOULOGNE (Troopship "HENRIETTE")	
BOULOGNE	"	13.30	BN arrives BOULOGNE and proceeds to Rest Camp (OSTROHOVE)	
Do	26/2/17	10 oc	A & D COYS entrain for SALEUX	
SALEUX	26/2/17	16 oc	do arrive SALEUX (+ billet for night)	
BOULOGNE	27/2/17	10 oc	B & C Coys entrain for SALEUX	
SALEUX	27/2/17	16 oc	do arrive SALEUX (+ billet for night)	

(Cont'd on Sheet 2)
Lt Colr. cmdg 2/6 Bn
N. STAFFS REGT

WAR DIARY
INTELLIGENCE SUMMARY

2/6TH BN. NORTH STAFFORD REGT.

VOLUME 3
Page 2.

Place	Date	Hour	Summary of Events and Information	Remarks and references to Appendices
LONGEAUX	27/2/17	14 a.m.	BN 1ST LINE TRANSPORT Bn joined up by A & D Coys, proceed by March route to FOUILLOY.	
FOUILLOY	27/2/17	19 a.m.	BN 1ST LINE TRANSPORT with A & D Coys arrive FOUILLOY and are billeted for the night.	J.H.F.
Do.	28/2/17	9.45	do. leave FOUILLOY and proceed by March route to MORCOURT.	
MORCOURT	28/2/17	16 o'c	do. arrive MORCOURT. Bn H.Q. established at the Mairie.	J.H.F.

(continued on Sheet 3)

J.H. Forster wsfr Lt.-Col.
Comdg 2/6TH N. STAFF. REGT.

Army Form C. 2118.

WAR DIARY

~~INTELLIGENCE SUMMARY~~

(Erase heading not required.)

Original

Vol II

Confidential

WAR DIARY.

of

2/6 Bn NORTH STAFFS REGT.

from - 1st March 1917   To 29th March 1917

VOLUME III

Army Form C. 2118.

VOLUME 3
Page 3.

WAR DIARY
INTELLIGENCE SUMMARY
(Erase heading not required.)

2/6TH BN. NORTH STAFFORD REGT.

Place	Date	Hour	Summary of Events and Information	Remarks and references to Appendices
MORCOURT	1/3/17	17.30	B & C Coys arrive and join up with Bn.	LH.T.
Do	2/3/17		Bn rests at MORCOURT.	LH.T.
Do	"	16oc	Advance party return from instructional tour in trenches and rejoin Bn.	
Do	3/2/17		12 Offrs 92 O.R. proceed to 1st Line Trenches.	LH.T.
Do	4/3/17		Lt-Col T.B.H.THORNE proceeds to FOUCAUCOURT. One platoon from A Company proceeds to FOUCAUCOURT (2/Lt COUCHMAN i/c) Strength Off 1 O.R. 38	LH.F. LH.F.
Do	6/3/17		Bn proceeds to FOUCAUCOURT. Strength 110, 452 O.R.	LH.F. LH.F.
FOUCAUCOURT	7/3/17	17-30	Bn relieves 1/5 Border Regt in front line trenches.	LH.F.
Do	"	21-50	Relief completed	LH.F.
TRENCHES	8/3/17	20.00	Casualties K. nil O.R. W. nil O. 1 O.R.	LH.F.
Do	9/3/17	20.00	Casualties K. nil O.R. W. nil O. 2 O.R.	LH.F.
Do	10/3/17	20.00	One platoon in each company of the 2/5 Bn SOUTH STAFFS. REGT. arrive for instruction and relieve corresponding platoons who proceed to BERNY in support.	LH.F.
Do	11/3/17	20.00	Bn relieved by 2/5 Bn SOUTH STAFFS REGT.	LH.F.
Do	"	23.20	Relief completed.	
BERNY			Bn proceeds into Support Trenches.	LH.F.
Do	14/3/17	24.00	Bn relieved by 2/5 Bn SOUTH STAFFS. REGT.	LH.F. 2/F.
Do	15/3/17	6.00	Relief complete	
FOUCAUCOURT	"		Bn reoccupy Rest Billets	
Do	"	17.30	Bn proceed to front line trenches and relieve 2/5 Bn SOUTH STAFFS REGT.	LH.F.
Do	"	23.30	Relief completed.	

continued on sheet 4

T.B. Forbes Maj. Lt-Col
Comdg 2/6 N. STAFFS. REGT.

Army Form C. 2118.

WAR DIARY
INTELLIGENCE SUMMARY
(Erase heading not required.)

2/6 Bn. NORTH STAFFS REGT.

VOLUME 3
page 4

Place	Date	Hour	Summary of Events and Information	Remarks and references to Appendices
TRENCHES	19/3/17	11·00	Bn receives orders to advance and occupy Enemy Support Line Trenches. Patrols sent out and report enemy having evacuated trenches	
Do	"	11·30	Bn advances in WAVES in attack formation	
Do	"	"	Bn shelled with shrapnel during advance	
Do	"	12·00	Casualties K Nil O.R. Nil W Nil O.R.	
Do	"	"	Enemy support line occupied and consolidation commenced	
Do	"	12·45	Orders received that advance is to be continued and final position to be taken up was CROCODILE TRENCH from EAST of MAZINCOURT VILLAGE along VILLERS-CARBONNEL-MARCHELEPOT ROAD and to gain touch with 2/4th LEICESTER REGT on the left (62c S.W.)	
Do	"	15·30	Position above occupied and consolidation commenced. Body of 1 O.R. previously reported missing found in German Trench	Lt.F. Lt.F.
MAZINCOURT	19/3/17	–	Patrols sent forward to River SOMME who report country in front clear of enemy	
Do	21·3·17	12·00	Bn receives orders to advance to a line POULE-VERTE TRENCH – ACTRICE TRENCH Bn Hd Qrs established on TROY – VILLERS-CARBONNEL ROAD at T12 d 4.5 (62c S.W.)	Lt.F.
MISERY	"	14·30	Line as above occupied	Lt.F.
Do	22·3·17	"	Notification received that Capt. H.E. CHERRY had been evacuated to England. Authority DAG's list No 103/705	Lt.F.
Do	25·3·17	14·00	Notification received that Capt. F.A. YEOMANS had been evacuated to England. Authority DAG's list No 106. Bn Hd Qrs moved to U 1 a 3·0 (62c S.W.)	Lt.F.
Do	28·3·17	9·00	Bn moves forward to ESTRÉES-EN-CHAUSSÉE	Lt.F.
ESTRÉES-EN-CHAUSSÉE	"	14·30	Bn arrive and is billeted in the village	
Do.	29·3·17	–	Bn rested at ESTRÉES-EN-CHAUSSÉE	

Lt.F. Noss, major
Comdg 2/6 N STAFFS REGT.

Army Form C. 2118.

WAR DIARY
INTELLIGENCE SUMMARY
(Erase heading not required.)

Vol 3

Original

Confidential

2/6th North Staffs Regt.

War Diary

From 1st April 1917.   To 30th April 1917.

Volume 3. pages 5 to 8.

Army Form C. 2118.

page 5

WAR DIARY
INTELLIGENCE SUMMARY

(Erase heading not required.)

Place	Date	Hour	Summary of Events and Information	Remarks and references to Appendices
BOUCLY	1-4-17	—	Increase in strength 2 Officers	Initials
"	2-4-17	8.00	Battalion moved to HAMELET. Headquarters established at K31 d 0.1 (62C Ed.1)	Initials
		18.00	Billeting completed	
"	3-4-17	8.30	Work commenced on Line of Defence. Right flank Q2 d 6.0. Left flank K19 a 7.7 (62C ED I)	Initials
"	5-4-17	20.00	Verbal instructions received from 176th Brigade H.Q. through Staff Captain that one company completely equipped for fighting was to proceed to HERVILLY to be attached to 75th N. Staff Regt.	
		22.00	"A" Offr. 129 OR. proceeded as above. They were sent to dig communication trenches	Initials
"	6-4-17	7.40	"B" Company as above returned to Hd Qrs.	
"	7-4-17	—	Increase in strength 2 Officers	Initials
"	8-4-17	10.00	Commanding Officer and Adjutant proceeded on reconnaissance with a view to attack on LE VERGUIER and FERVAQUE FARM	
		17.00	MAJOR PORTER instructed to take over temporary command of the 75th S Staff Regt and proceeded at once	
		22.00	C.O. and Adjt returned from reconnaissance and held a conference. Instructions were issued that the Bn should act as Brigade Reserve with Hd Qrs at HERVILLY	Initials
"	9-4-17	10.00	Verbal instructions received from BGC that attack cancelled. Bn to 'stand to' for move.	
		17.30	Bn proceeded to HERVILLY. Headquarters established at K23 d H 3 (sheet 62 c NE)	
		20.00	Billeting completed	
HERVILLY		22.00	C.O. placed in command of 75th N Staff Regt in addition to his Bn, and ordered to push forward one company to Divisional Line in GRAND PRIEL WOOD with Bns on right and left flanks.	Initials
"	10-4-17	5.45	"B" Coy takes up position in GRAND PRIEL WOOD to gain touch on Right with 76th S Staff Regt and on left with 75th Leicester Regt. Increase in strength 5 I.O.R.	Initials

continued on page 6.

WAR DIARY
or
INTELLIGENCE SUMMARY

Army Form C. 2118.

page 6.

Place	Date	Hour	Summary of Events and Information	Remarks and references to Appendices
HERVILLY	10.4.17	5:45	'D' Company sent forward to construct shelters in Devencourt Lower Resistance Line owing to observation from enemy lines. 'D' Company were withdrawn from vacated German line	
JEANCOURT		14.00	Orders received for Battalion to move to JEANCOURT.	
		20.30	Bn (less B Coy on outpost duty) completely billeted.	
	11.4.17	14.00	'B' Company relieved by 2/4 Leicesters. went to England.	
	13.4.17	00.00	B & C Companies of this unit relieve 2 companies of 2/6 S. Staff Regt in support line. Decrease in strength 2/Lt F. BENNION	2/4F
			Remaining companies of 'D' each assisted by 50 men from companies in support line advanced and occupied GRAND PRIEL and ASCENCION FARMS. The company occupying ASCENCION FARM was held up for a short time by M.G. fire, eventually driving out the enemy from the position with bombs	2/4F
	14.4.17	7:45	A & D Companies proceeded to consolidate their respective objectives with strong posts during the morning. ASCENCION FARM was heavily shelled with H.E. and shrapnel	2/4F
			Astrong post was dug at L.35.b.3.7 (sheet 62cNE) which was occupied by one platoon with an officer.	2/4F
	15.4.17		ASCENCION FARM heavily shelled during morning. Casualties K. Off. NIL OR. 1 W. Off. 1 OR. 1 Missing 1 OR. 1 however in strength 1 officer.	2/4F
L.28.a.5.4 (Sheet 62cNE)	16.4.17	20.30	Bn. HQ moved from JEANCOURT and established in QUARRY at L.29.a.5.4 (sheet 62cNE) Bn. relieved in Old German Line by 2/6 & 2/4 S. Staff Regts and then advanced and dug in on a new line of 6 strong posts running from ASCENCION FARM - GRAND PRIEL FARM - CHATEAU	2/4F
	17.4.17	16.00	GRAND PRIEL FARM shelled during afternoon.	2/4F
		20.30	Bn relieved by 2/6 S. Staff Regt and occupied old German trench W of LE VERGUIER with advance posts running E. of LE VERGUIER.	2/4F

continued on page 7.

Army Form C. 2118.

page 7

WAR DIARY
or
INTELLIGENCE SUMMARY
(Erase heading not required.)

Instructions regarding War Diaries and Intelligence Summaries are contained in F. S. Regs., Part II. and the Staff Manual respectively. Title Pages will be prepared in manuscript.

Place	Date	Hour	Summary of Events and Information	Remarks and references to Appendices
JEANCOURT	17.4.17	20.30	Bn H.Q. established at JEANCOURT. Relief complete. Casualties K.Off Nil OR Nil W.Off Nil OR 2	Appx
	18.4.17	1.00		Appx
	19.4.17		Casualties K.Off Nil OR Nil W.Off Nil OR 2	Appx
	20.4.17		Casualties K.Off Nil OR Nil W.Off Nil OR 3. Increase of strength 2 Off. 10 OR.	Appx
	21.4.17	20.30	Bn. relieved the S. Staff Regt in advanced line in front of ASCENCION FARM and GRAND PRIEL FARM. A & D Companies with 2 platoons of B Company attached; platoon to S & C Companies respectively on the flanks of the Bn frontage) organised in depth in front and local support lines. Remaining 2 platoons of B company in reserve occupy Devereaux Mess House + line of Resistance. Casualties K.Off Nil OR Nil W.Off Nil OR 3.	Appx 1
	22.4.17	21.30	Two patrols each of 1 Off. + 10 H+ 16 OR proceeded from GRAND PRIEL and ASCENCION FARMS respectively to reconnoitre position called ARTILLERY TREE (L.24 e.35 about 62ᶜNE) and then to proceed to L.24 e.5.6 and from there in a S.E. direction to L.30 a.9.4 which line was supposed to be a line of German rifle pits. The patrol from GRAND PRIEL FARM was heavily fired on when they got to within 10 yards of the TREE but obtained the desired information and withdrew. Casualties K.Off Nil OR 3 W.Off Nil OR 2. 3 Officers in Strength.	Appx
	23.4.17	21.30	Advanced posts dug on line L.24 e.3.8 (about 62ᶜNE) and G.25 d.5.5 (about 62ᶜBNW) at G.26 d.3-4 (ad 62ᶜBNW.) L.30c.9.8, L.24 d.4.3 (ad 62ᶜNE) Position at L.24 c.4.3 taken after considerable resistance and consolidated. Casualties K.Off Nil OR Nil W.Off Nil OR 16.	Appx
	24.4.17	20.30	Advanced posts established previous night heavily shelled by enemy during day & carried out and intermediate posts constructed Consolidation of advanced posts at L.30 a 6.6 and L.24 a 2.3 (about 62ᶜNE)	Appx

Continued on page 8.

Army Form C. 2118.

page 8.

WAR DIARY
~~INTELLIGENCE SUMMARY~~
(Erase heading not required.)

Instructions regarding War Diaries and Intelligence Summaries are contained in F. S. Regs., Part II. and the Staff Manual respectively. Title Pages will be prepared in manuscript.

Place	Date	Hour	Summary of Events and Information	Remarks and references to Appendices
JEANCOURT	25/4/17	—	Advanced posts again heavily shelled by enemy casualties K. Off Nil OR Nil W/Off. CAPT. H.G. WAGHORN (out of wounds 26/4/17) OR 1.	W.H.F.
		21:30	Bn relieved by 2/6th S. Staff Regt and on completion of relief occupy Divisional Reserve Line of resistance E. of LE VERGUIER and support trench	W.H.F.
	26/4/17	16:30	Old German trench W of LE VERGUIER heavily shelled by enemy	W.H.F.
	27/4/17		Bn to be relieved by 1/4 Leicester Regt this date	W.H.F.
		11:00	Relief postponed 24 hours.	W.H.F.
	28/4/17	4:00	Bn relieved by 1/4 Leicester Regt and on completion proceeded to Nob Bullets in BERNES.	W.H.F.
BERNES	29/4/17	18:00	Relief completed and H. Qrs established at Q.10.a.9.9. (sht 62°S.E.)	W.H.F.
	30/4/17		Strength of Battalion Officers 39 O.R. 785.	W.H.F.

B.M. Thorne Lt. Col.
Commdg. 2/6 Bn North Staffs Regt.

Army Form C. 2118.

WAR DIARY
or
INTELLIGENCE SUMMARY

(Erase heading not required.)

Instructions regarding War Diaries and Intelligence Summaries are contained in F. S. Regs., Part II and the Staff Manual respectively. Title Pages will be prepared in manuscript.

Place	Date	Hour	Summary of Events and Information	Remarks and references to Appendices

Original

Vol 4

Confidential

War Diary
of
2/6th North Stafford Regiment

From :- 1st May, 1917
To :- 31st May, 1917

Army Form C. 2118.

WAR DIARY
or
INTELLIGENCE SUMMARY

(Erase heading not required.)

Instructions regarding War Diaries and Intelligence Summaries are contained in F.S. Regs., Part II. and the Staff Manual respectively. Title Pages will be prepared in manuscript.

Page 9

Place	Date	Hour	Summary of Events and Information	Remarks and references to Appendices
BERNES	1-5-17	9.30	Length of Bn. H.Q. 40 Bn 653. Orders received that the Bn., Bn Stores and transport were to move to NOBESCOURT FARM (224.2.9.9)(62.9 NE)	Appx
		10.30	Bn inspected by G.O.C. before bnfg Bks.	Appx
		14.00	Bn and 8th Lanes move to NOBESCOURT FARM and H.Q. established at 224d.9.9 (sheet 62.9 NE) Bn billeted in tents.	
NOBESCOURT FARM	2.5.17		Transport lines moved to NOBESCOURT FARM from BERNES	
	3.5.17	10.30	Transport inspected by 406 Major bef. Bde.	
	6.5.17	19.30	Bn never H.Q. to relieve a Bn. of the 99th bef. Bde in the left subsector of the Divl left sector.	
L.10.A.6.4			Bn. HQ. established at L.10.a.6.4 (sheet 62.9.NE).	
			9th Lanes and transport move from NOBESCOURT FARM to ROISEL.	
	7.5.17	3.55	Bn relieves 20th Bn Sherwood Yeomen in the left subsector of the Divl left sector. Casualties K.H.H NIL, O.H NIL, W.H.H NIL B.O 1.	
		21.30	'A' & 'B' Coys 276.X sent staff kept relieved by 'A' & 'A' Coys 4th Lines kept and on completion of relief 'O' Coy relieves 'A' H.Q. and 'B' & 'B' Coy reliever 'B' Coy on the SWITCH TRENCH. 'B' Coy then withdrawn to Bn H.Q. 'A' or 'D' Coys met at Bn H.Q. in shelters prior to making an attack on German frontier the following night. Patrols sent out from 'A', 'B' Coys to reconnoitre position to be attacked. Patrol heavily fined on by enemy on nearing their wire. Casualties K.H.H. H.S 2, W.H.H NIL B.O 2.	
	8.5.17	21.50	L.6.a 2.0 (sheet 62.9 NE) 'A' & 'B' Coys and F.3.0 & (sheet 62.B.NW) and UN-NAMED FARM at Objectives :-	Appx
			'A' Coy L.6.a 5.5 to L.6.a 5.9.	
			'B' " L.6.a 5.9 to F.30. 0.24	
			'C' UN-NAMED FARM L.6.a.2.0	
			Attacking troops were met by very heavy M.G. fire, one platoon 'A' Coy under Lieut P.G. Holman with 15 M's reached their Objective and consolidated it, meeting several flanking attacks from both flanks.	

(continued on Page 10)

Army Form C. 2118.

Page 10

WAR DIARY
or
INTELLIGENCE SUMMARY
(Erase heading not required.)

Instructions regarding War Diaries and Intelligence Summaries are contained in F.S. Regs., Part II. and the Staff Manual respectively. Title Pages will be prepared in manuscript.

Place	Date	Hour	Summary of Events and Information	Remarks and references to Appendices
L10a6.4	8.5.14	24.00	'A' & 'B' Coys less 1 platoon did not reach their objective. UN-NAMED FARM reoccupied by E Coy after very heavy shelling. Casualties:- Missing believed killed Offs - Lieut M.B. GRACE, Lieut R.L. CANBY, 2/Lieut C.S. COUCHMAN. O.Rs - 28 Killed Offs - NIL O.Rs - 2 Died of Wounds Offs - NIL O.Rs - 1 Wounded Offs - CAPT. G.D. CHARLTON, LIEUT P.G. COLEMAN, 2/LIEUT F.E. BURT, 2/LIEUT C.J.G. FRYER (N.Staffs Regt attached 2nd North Staffs Regt) 2/LIEUT W. JOHNSON (at duty) O.Rs - 42.	Off.
	9.5.14	10.0	UN-NAMED FARM heavily shelled.	
		21.00	The platoon of 'B' Coy under LIEUT. COLEMAN which had reached its objective was attacked several times during the day and previous night by German bombing up the trench, and after using all their supply of S.A.A. and bombs, LIEUT COLEMAN used German bombs which he found, and repeatedly fielded up German stick bombs which had been thrown at his party and threw them back at the Germans.	
		22.30	The platoon of 'B' Coy under LIEUT COLEMAN withdrew from the German trench which they had held during the day after having defended all fall and bombs. They were charged by the Germans previous to withdrawing but met their bayonets with great effect. LIEUT COLEMAN was again wounded (in the mouth) with a fragment of a bomb just before he withdrew from the German trench.	L.H.H.
	10.5.14	22.00	Bn relieved by 2/4th South Staffs Regt in the Left Subsector of the Left Sector of the Division.	L.H.H.
ROISEL	11.5.14	2.00	Bn H.Q. established at ROISEL K16d 2.8 (Sheet 62cNE)	L.H.H.

(continued on page 11)

2449 Wt. W14957/Mgo 750,000 1/16 J.B.C. & A. Forms/C.2118/12.

WAR DIARY
or
INTELLIGENCE SUMMARY
(Erase heading not required.)

Army Form C. 2118.

Page 11

Place	Date	Hour	Summary of Events and Information	Remarks and references to Appendices
ROISEL	11.5.17	16:40	Bn inspected by G.O.C. 59th Division who congratulated the Bn for the good march performed on the night of the 8th/9th inst.	
	12.5.17		Congratulatory telegram received from Corps Commander.	2/LH
L10a 6.H	14.5.17	22:0	Entered in strength H.H. 1 O.R. NIL. Bn relieves 9th South Staff Regt in the left subsector of the Divl left sector.	5/LH 2/LH
	15.5.17		Increase in strength H.H. 1 O.R. NIL	2/LH 2/LH
	16.5.17		Casualties K H NIL W H NIL O.R. NIL	
	18.5.17		" K H NIL W H NIL O.R. 1	2/LH
	19.5.17	24:00	Bn relieved by 2/6th South Staff Regt in the left subsector of the Divl left sector.	2/LH
ROISEL	20.5.17	4.00	Casualties K H NIL W H NIL O.R. 1	5/LH
			Bn HQ started in ROISEL K16 d.2.F (sheet 62 d NE).	
VILLERS FAUCON	23.5.17	15:40	Bn with transport and gun teams moves to VILLERS FAUCON	2/LH
		19:30	Bn HQ established E.22 b.4.0 (Sheet 62 d NE)	2/LH 2/LH
	28.5.17		Increase in strength O.H. NIL O.R. 45	
	29.5.17		" " " H.H. 1 O.R. NIL	
			Notification received of the following awards:-	
			CROIX DE GUERRE 2/Lt (temp Lieut) EDWARD RIDGWAY	
			DISTINGUISHED SERVICE ORDER 2/Lt (temp Lieut) P.G. COLEMAN	
	30.5.17		MILITARY MEDAL No 241089 L/Cpl POYNTON W.H.	
			Notification received of the following award :-	
			MILITARY CROSS 2/Lt G.J.G. FRYER (9th West Lanc. Regt)	2/LH
EQUANCOURT	31.5.17	18:42	Bn leaves VILLERS FAUCON and proceeds via SOREL LE GRAND – FINS – EQUANCOURT.	
		21:45	Bn arrives EQUANCOURT and goes into camp at VIIaD.11 (between road & railway) (sheet 57b SE)	2/LH

B.R. Thorne Lt-Col.
Comdg. 2/6 Bn North Staffs Regt.

Army Form C. 2118.

WAR DIARY
or
INTELLIGENCE SUMMARY

(Erase heading not required.)

Vol 5

Original

Confidential

War Diary
of
2/6th North Stafford Regiment
From:- 1st June 1917
To:- 30th June 1917

WAR DIARY
or
INTELLIGENCE SUMMARY

(Erase heading not required.)

Army Form C. 2118.

Place	Date	Hour	Summary of Events and Information	Remarks and references to Appendices
EQUANCOURT	1.6.17		Fighting Strength H/40 32/1143 2/Lt. A.H.C. Palmer joined from England.	O/C
	2.6.17	13.30	Bn and transport moved to new camp at W10 b 1.2 (Sheet 57 b 6 SE)	O/C
	3.6.17		Draft of 130 arrived for the Bn.	O/C
	4.6.17		Training carried out in vicinity of Camp.	O/C
	5.6.17		"A" "B" "D" Coys to NEUVILLE for work on NEUVILLE – METZ Road. 2/Lt W.P. Hunt and 2/Lt. joined the Bn.	O/C
	9.6.17	19/45	1/Lt Hance & 4 Patrouns N.B. Jones and 260 Hellcons joined from England.	O/C
			"A" "B" + "D" Coys relieved 2/R NEUVILLE left 2 Coys 1st Bn Staffs left and returned to Camp.	O/C
	10.6.17		day of Platoon Commanders attached to 2/Bn Dismount Voices on the Line for the Bn.	O/C
	11.6.17	10.20	"B" Coy moved off to relieve "B" Coy 2/Rd Dismount Yorkies in the Dismount Line.	O/C
		19.30	Bn. less "B" Coy leave EQUANCOURT to relieve 2/7th Dismount Yorkies on the Line. Disposition as follows "A" + "D" Coys to front line and followed thus "D" Coy in support and "B" Coy in reserve	O/C
	12.6.17	3.0	Relief complete. The U.S. S 10 a 4.9 (Sheet 57 B L.E.) Coy new H.Q's from front line dismount. Gunthorbs O.Pos W.I. Line 10 B A frost 2rdn Lt Young and 2/Lt Yates joined from England.	O/C
	13.6.17		Work on front line system continues Casualties (see B 2 W.J.)	O/C

WAR DIARY or INTELLIGENCE SUMMARY

Army Form C. 2118.

(Erase heading not required.)

Instructions regarding War Diaries and Intelligence Summaries are contained in F.S. Regs., Part II. and the Staff Manual respectively. Title Pages will be prepared in manuscript.

Place	Date	Hour	Summary of Events and Information	Remarks and references to Appendices
B10.d.2.8	16.6.17		'A' & 'B' Coys relieved in Front Line by 'C' & 'D' Coys, 'B' Coy going into support and 'A' Coy to the intermediate line. Casualties 2/O. W.I.	OC
	17.6.17	8.15	Inter Company Relief completed. Casualties O/R. W.H. (2/Cpl accidentally wounded by rifleman of a Lewis gunner.)	OC
	15.6.17		Fixing up of Advance Posts completed and new Front Line and extension throughout. I new O.P. completed from rest to new Front Line. Disposition of Coys now as follows:- Front Line and Forward support 'C' & 'D' Coys. Forward Reserve 'A' Coy. Reserve 'B' Coy.	OC
				OC
	19.6.17		Very heavy rain. Trenches waterlogged. Casualties O/R W.I.	
	20.6.17		Rained intermittently throughout day.	OC
	21.6.17		All available men working on draining and clearing of trenches.	
	22.6.17		Bn. relieved in Front Line by 7/R.W. Regt. and proceeded to billets at NEUVILLE	OC
P22.b.9.1	23.6.17	3.0	Relief completed and Bn. in billets. Weather warmer. Bn. HQ P22.b.9.1 (57d SE) Working party 42 Coys found for work on front line system, duties all ranks	OC
	24.6.17		— do —	OC
	25.6.17		— do —	OC
	24.6.17		— do —	OC
				OC
	25.6.17		Nothing heavy. Parades continued owing to violent thunderstorm.	OC
	26.6.17		Usual working party found. Casualties 2/O W.I.	OC

Army Form C. 2118.

WAR DIARY
or
INTELLIGENCE SUMMARY

(Erase heading not required.)

Vol 6

Confidential

War Diary
of
2/6th North Stafford Regiment

From 1st July 1917
To 31st July 1917

Place	Date	Hour	Summary of Events and Information	Remarks and references to Appendices
Original				

Army Form C. 2118.

WAR DIARY
or
INTELLIGENCE SUMMARY

(Erase heading not required.)

Instructions regarding War Diaries and Intelligence Summaries are contained in F. S. Regs., Part II. and the Staff Manual respectively. Title Pages will be prepared in manuscript.

Place	Date	Hour	Summary of Events and Information	Remarks and references to Appendices
			Lighting Strength Return 44/39 7/6 7/19	
M6 B 1.2	1.4.19	10.45	On march to camp at EQUANCOURT. Divisional Reserve. An HQ established at V16.5.1.2 (54½ S.R.)	App 1
	2.4.19		1 M. and 19880 proceeded as advance party to mark out site of New camp in W. Loops Reserve. Recce that YDB Horse assumed command of 1/6 Bn Rbs during absence of Brig. Genl. Rob Barnes D.S.O. in leave	App 1
		23.20	Gas alarm. Battalion stood to and alarm cancelled at 23.40.	App 1
	14.4.19	1.40	" " " " " 1.45.	App 1
	4.4.19	6.20am	Bn, QM Stores and Transport moved by march route via LECHELLE and BUS to new Brigade Camp. An HQ established at O.10.c.3.5.	App 1
O.10.c.3.5	5.4.19 to 12.4.19		Training carried out in vicinity of Camp.	App 1
	23.4.19		Bn took part in Rde Trident Exercise (moves to Trench attack).	App 1
	24.4.19		Bn took part in Div Trident Exercise (German Trenches between H.1.d.4.2 and H.36.a.4.2, 54½ S.W.) to which Bn Horse to Brigade ride.	App 1
			Casualties during month	
			NIL	

M.W. Cokewalle Capt
Comdg 1/6 W.Staffs Regt

Army Form C. 2118.

WAR DIARY
or
INTELLIGENCE SUMMARY
(Erase heading not required.)

Instructions regarding War Diaries and Intelligence Summaries are contained in F. S. Regs., Part II. and the Staff Manual respectively. Title Pages will be prepared in manuscript.

Place	Date	Hour	Summary of Events and Information	Remarks and references to Appendices
			Original	Vol 7

Confidential

War Diary
of
2/6th Bn North Staffordshire Regiment

From 1st Aug 1917
To 31st Aug 1917

Army Form C. 2118.

WAR DIARY
or
INTELLIGENCE SUMMARY.

(Erase heading not required.)

Instructions regarding War Diaries and Intelligence Summaries are contained in F. S. Regs., Part II. and the Staff Manual respectively. Title pages will be prepared in manuscript.

Place	Date	Hour	Summary of Events and Information	Remarks and references to Appendices
HAPLINCOURT	8/9/14		Order to 4th Bn received from Bde.	R.1
	10/9/14		2 Coys 4th Bn sent to Ameins to support detachments there	R.2
	11/9/14		Orders (verbal to Coms. 10 inch 27/M.86)	R.3
	13/9/14		Order of 10 Bde received from Bde.	R.4
	14/9/14		2 Coys of 4th Bn arrived at Amens. No supplies of 4th Yrs today	R.5
	15/9/14		Order of 10 Bde received from Bde.	R.6
	17/9/14		Bn moved out to the back on Our Corner however fresh Hill hopital returned within	R.7
	19/9/14	a.m.	Bn relieved from Back Corner	R.8
	19/9/14	a.m.	Order of 10 Bde received from Bde.	R.9
			Several parties under Major C.H. Kelly proceeded to BAPAUME to roll up material	
			holding arrangements for Bn proceeding to-morrow	
	25/9/14	6.35	Bn moved to Ausheux; arrived 7.30 H to sqdn 13 4 to 5.30 B H 7 (field) 9 orders and ALBERT arrived	R.10
			had [?] after 60 branches and proceeded to find accommodation at FRENCUILLE arrived 8 a.m.	
FRENCUILLE	24/9/14	12 a.m.	Orders of 4th Bn received from Bde not needed to Bde.	R.11
	25/9/14		Preliminary instructions received from Commander-in-Chief W. Corps [?] Slater	R.12
	25/9/14		Advance party under 4th Division located to new area	R.13
	26/9/14	11.00	Operation orders received from Brigade for movement of ADVN to H.Q. for M. morning	R.14
	26/9/14	20.15	4 day rations to be carried out for men in Brigade Group	R.15
	27/9/14	p.m.	Bn less 2 Coys arrived at AVELUY to QH to forming for M. Aq[?] to HAMEL	

Army Form C. 2118.

WAR DIARY
or
INTELLIGENCE SUMMARY.
(Erase heading not required.)

17/59 Vol 8

Instructions regarding War Diaries and Intelligence Summaries are contained in F. S. Regs., Part II. and the Staff Manual respectively. Title pages will be prepared in manuscript.

Place	Date	Hour	Summary of Events and Information	Remarks and references to Appendices

Confidential

Original War Diary
of
2/6th Bn. North Stafford Regiment

From 1st Sept 1917
To 30th Sept 1917

Army Form C. 2118.

WAR DIARY
or
INTELLIGENCE SUMMARY.
(Erase heading not required.)

Instructions regarding War Diaries and Intelligence Summaries are contained in F. S. Regs., Part II. and the Staff Manual respectively. Title pages will be prepared in manuscript.

Place	Date	Hour	Summary of Events and Information	Remarks and references to Appendices
	18/9/14	10.40	An order ordered march of Division	O.C.
		11.50	Bn. lien 9th Bay marched by manh route in 1 ARGLE and STENWOORDE to WINNEZEELE was escort of heavy luggage leaving practically with baggage 15 lbs. per man.	O.C.
WINNEZEELE	19/9/14		Usual fatigue parties and drills in vicinity of camp.	O.C.
	20/9/14		Fatigues etc.	O.C.
	21/9/14	9.30	Whole force again split. C Coy. proceeded by bus to ENTRANCHT etc.	O.C.
		10.50	The remainder and trained to FRONT Pgs B &D (3000 men) left by rail at 11 where 2 orders to embark for.	O.C.
			Bn. detrained at 8.15. and marched to depot at BAILLEUL where whole remained inactivity an account of bad weather on arrival. rest of Bn arrived at 11 m'le rails noted destination to front at day	O.C.
	22/9/14		Bn. in readiness to move all day.	
		9.30	Bn. left for front. Everything ok, its no be moved up in lorries belonging to Lon. to Anti. 1 mile N.W. of KLAYER HOEPE which came under fire of late arty. (Par Herr.)	O.C.
	23/9/14		Bn. in trenches all day. Casualties 60 wounded.	O.C.
	24/9/14	10.30	Bn. moved up to sept. front line in front of Meters and west of Ealarge Liverpool trenches 200 yards + north of	O.C.
	25/9/14	19.30	Hostile gun shell burst rabould between 1.30-19pm 11.50 made on wpt. it appears to	O.C.
			have offered of fire	

Army Form C. 2118.

WAR DIARY
or
INTELLIGENCE SUMMARY.
(Erase heading not required.)

Instructions regarding War Diaries and Intelligence Summaries are contained in F. S. Regs., Part II. and the Staff Manual respectively. Title pages will be prepared in manuscript.

Place	Date	Hour	Summary of Events and Information	Remarks and references to Appendices
	23/9/17	22.00	Bn marched up into front line relieving units of 55 Divn. Bn relieved positions thereabouts Officer Killed 1 (2/Lt ?? Amid) Bty wounded 1	α.
	24/9/17	23.00	Bn received heavy shell fire from 4.30 – 6.30am Bn relieved in front line by M.G. Bn/Bde and marched to camp back at N.W. LAMKERTINGHE The mother in camp during day Casualties: Other ranks 1 wounded 9 missing 9	α. α.
	25/9/17	10.20	Bn moved up into 2nd Reserve MGR and MYR held in front line. Officers Killed and sick	α.
			Herd in Reserve	α.
		3.50	Air artillery fire seems very heavy barrage as preparation for J.A. One platoon withdrawn	α.
		6.00	MYR and HMR Bde reserve with 2/9 Bn to move out 26th Road in the support	α.
		08.00	Information received that all positions taken with several slight casualties	α.
		18.45	Information received that Divn on right flank of 39 Divn has been wounded attacks and slightly driven in. Bn immediately ordered up and required to return if no further action of present accord	α.
			on CAPRICORN (unclear) BUS. Bn HQ in CAPRICORN KEEP (hereabouts Officers wounded 1 (2/Lt W Thurston) other ranks Killed 2 wounded 21 (inferred)	α.
	26/9/17	22.30	Bn HQ remain until 22 Anterior Hereabout the day after severe action. Bn (2nd in platoon left in EASTACORN TRENCHES) Officers 2/Lt JULIEN (2/Lt party to 9 Bde Bdes) moved up to front line for train	α.
	27/9/17	11.30	Battalion HQ established in trench dugout CLUSTER HOUSES	α.
		4.00	Relief complete	α.
		6-6.30	Hostile barrage 6.15 on Mostly shallow intermittent shell fire in rear	α.
			Attack reported to have been very successful, unconfirmed, Hostile hostile artillery throughout the day	α.

WAR DIARY
or
INTELLIGENCE SUMMARY

Army Form C. 2118.

(Erase heading not required.)

Place	Date	Hour	Summary of Events and Information	Remarks and references to Appendices
	27/9/17	K-8:38	[illegible] shelling and machine gun fire inflicted casualties.	or
	28/9/17	2.00	Heavy hostile gas shell bombardment. Approx. 2000 shells upon our position. No casualties.	or
		13.30	Our HQ dugout heavily bombarded with 5.9" shells. No direct hits on dugouts but several damage. Hostile shelling from Western slopes	or
		20.00	Relief of the 5th [illegible] by 7th [illegible] commenced	or
		24.30	Relief completed. 7th [illegible] took over the line. [illegible] many bombs dropped. Casualties due to enemy shelling during day, three wounded 1 (O.R. officer) 6th [illegible] ranks killed, wounded 12. [illegible] 21 1 died [illegible] casualties occurred on 2 platoon	or
	29/9/17		left billets in CAPRICORN TRENCHES for rest in camp.	or

Army Form C. 2118.

WAR DIARY
or
INTELLIGENCE SUMMARY

(Erase heading not required.)

Vol 9

Confidential

Original
War Diary
at
2/6th North Staffs Regiment

From: 1st Oct 1917
To: 31st Oct 1917

Army Form C. 2118.

WAR DIARY
or
INTELLIGENCE SUMMARY.
(Erase heading not required.)

Instructions regarding War Diaries and Intelligence Summaries are contained in F.S. Regs., Part II. and the Staff Manual respectively. Title pages will be prepared in manuscript.

Place	Date	Hour	Summary of Events and Information	Remarks and references to Appendices
ISBERGUES	1/10/17	8.00	Battalion marched to VLAMERTINGHE Stn and entrained at 10.15 am	nil
		10.20	Bn detrained at STEENBECQUE and marched to billets at ISBERGUES	nil
	2/10/17		Day spent in resting and cleaning up generally.	nil
	3/10/17		Cleaning up and training.	nil
	4/10/17		Orders received that Battalion is to move to BONY area	nil
PREDEFIN	7/10/17	8.15	Battalion moved by road and train en route to PREDEFIN. Heavy Rain	nil
	8/10/17		Day spent in cleaning up & c.	nil
	9/10/17	10.30	Orders received to be prepared to move on 10/10/17.	nil
	10/10/17	16.00	Battalion moved by bus onwards route to MARQUETTES FARM near BOUVIGNY. A reconnoitring party consisting of the four Company Commanders and Majors dealing made a tour of that part of the line which was intended to be taken over by the Battalion	nil
	11/10/17		Day spent in cleaning up. Commanding Officer held an inspection of clothing and kit	nil
	12/10/17	9.15	Battalion marched to FOSSE 10 and occupied the billets vacated by the 15th North Staffs Regt	nil
	13/10/17	18.00	Battalion marched to LIEVIN and relieved the 76th South Staffs Regt in support line. Relief completed 12.15.	nil
LIEVIN	14/10/17 21.		Battalion rested in day time and formed working and carrying parties at night.	nil
			The Battalion was subjected to heavy battle shelling. Casualties 1 OR wounded.	nil
	22/10/17	18.00	Battalion moved from Support line to relieve the 1/5th North Staffs Regt in front line. Relief completed 22.30	nil
	23/10/17		C Company relieved quiet. Casualties nil.	nil
	24/10/17		Situation shelling - Casualties nil	nil
	25/10/17		Hostile shelling. HQ relief. Casualties surrendered. 1 Officer (2/Lt E. Barnes) and 2 ORs	nil
	26/10/17		Station normal. B Company relief in place.	nil
			Enemy attempted an unsuccessful raid on two of our forward posts but were driven off. Our Casualties were 1 wounded O.R.	4.
	27/10/17	5.30	Capt/Lt R. C. Ironson assumed Command of the Battalion temporarily. Col Browning having been admitted to hospital	nil
			Major Ottleham leaves Battalion temporarily to take Command of the 7/5th South Staffs Regt	nil
			Capt Whittley able as 2nd in Command of Battalion	nil
			Situation quiet except for a little hostile shelling. Casualties nil	nil
	28/10/17		Battalion relieved by 7/5 Leicestershire Regiment and marched to ALBERTA Camp. SOUCHEZ	nil
SOUCHEZ	29/10/17		Battalion resting	nil
	30/10/17		Battalion found working parties.	nil
	31/10/17			nil

1/11/17

W.J. Maj.
M. Smith Stafford Regt Capt.

Army Form C. 2118.

WAR DIARY
or
INTELLIGENCE SUMMARY.

(Erase heading not required.)

Instructions regarding War Diaries and Intelligence Summaries are contained in F. S. Regs., Part II. and the Staff Manual respectively. Title pages will be prepared in manuscript.

Vol 10

Place	Date	Hour	Summary of Events and Information	Remarks and references to Appendices
Original			War Diary of 16TH North Lancs Regiment from 1st Nov 1914 to 30th Nov 1917	Incomplete

Army Form C. 2118.

WAR DIARY
or
INTELLIGENCE SUMMARY.
(Erase heading not required.)

Instructions regarding War Diaries and Intelligence Summaries are contained in F. S. Regs., Part II. and the Staff Manual respectively. Title pages will be prepared in manuscript.

Place	Date 1917	Hour	Summary of Events and Information	Remarks and references to Appendices
SOUCHEZ	18.7.		The following N.C.O. and men were presented with awards for Gallantry on the peld, when the Batt. was at YPRES. Military Medals to Cpl. Power, Ptes. Adams and Burke. Gallantry Cards to Col. Newman, Coleman, Lyle, Gun, Tolen & Pte. Westlands. The presentation was made by the G.O.C. Division.	M.S.
	5.		Orders received for the Battalion to move into the line.	M.S.
	6.		The Battalion relieved the 76 Sherwood Foresters in the left support trenches of the AVION sector, relief complete 12.a.m.	M.S.
			Capt. W. Hislop Lieut. Hubball awarded the Military Cross.	M.S.
	7.12		18th Tour working parties.	
	.12		Lt. Col. F.F. Keating assumes command of Battn. on his return from the 1/5 South Staffs Regt.	M.S.
AVION.	13. 14		Batt. relieved the 1/5 North Staffs Regt. in the left front line of the AVION sector, relief complete 11·30 p.m. This sector was very quiet and no casualties of any description occurred during the 7 days that the Battn. was in this part of the line.	M.S.
SOUCHEZ	17.18		The 15th Canadian Regiment relieved the Battalion which proceeded by train and march route back to ALBERTA CAMP.	M.S.
	19.		The Bn. left ALBERTA CAMP by march route to SIMONCOURT.	M.S.
SIMONCOURT	20		Orders were received to proceed to the COURCELLES area 30 minutes after the receipt of the codeword "BAPAUME". The Battalion stand to.	M.S.
	21.		The Bn. stands to all day until 11·30 pm when they proceeded to COURCELLES. LE COMTE arriving there at 5·30 am on the 22nd.	M.S.
ACHIET	22		The Bn. again stands to waiting for orders to move forward.	M.S.
	23	2 pm	The Bn. proceed by march route to ACHIET LE GRAND and there entrained for FINS and marched to HEUDICOURT arriving there 12 o'c midnight.	M.S.
HEUDICOURT				

WAR DIARY
or
INTELLIGENCE SUMMARY.

(Erase heading not required.)

Army Form C. 2118.

Instructions regarding War Diaries and Intelligence Summaries are contained in F. S. Regs., Part II. and the Staff Manual respectively. Title pages will be prepared in manuscript.

Place	Date 1917	Hour	Summary of Events and Information	Remarks and references to Appendices
HEUDICOURT	Nov 27	12.30pm	The Bn. holds itself in readiness to move forward at an hours notice.	
	27		The Bn. moves by march route to bivouac by FLESQUIRES relieving the 3rd Coldstream Guards.	
CAMBRAI FRONT	28		The Battalion takes over the front line system in BOURLON WOOD relieving the Welsh Guards	
	29		Our position heavily shelled by the enemy – Casualties 1-3 ; 13 and 29	
	30		The Battalion again heavily shelled especially "D" Coy where casualties were very heavy. Casualties 2-10 ; 29-237 In his bombardment the enemy used shrapnel and minenwerfer gasshells, and despite heavy casualties the Battalion still holds the line.	

Bernard Thurlow
Major

Army Form C. 2118.

WAR DIARY
or
INTELLIGENCE SUMMARY.
(Erase heading not required.)

Vol 11

Original

Confidential

War Diary

of

2/1st & 1/6th North Staffs Regiment

From 1st Dec 1917

To 31st Dec 1917

WAR DIARY
or
INTELLIGENCE SUMMARY.
(Erase heading not required.)

Army Form C. 2118.

Place	Date	Hour	Summary of Events and Information	Remarks and references to Appendices
BOURLON WOOD	Dec 1		On the night of the 1st-2nd the Battalion was relieved by the 7th Lincoln Regt and proceeded to the sunken road N.E. of FLESQUIERES	
FLESQUIERES	2		The 27 Nth Derby Regt took over the sunken road and the Battalion moved to FLESQUIERES	
	4		The Battalion was relieved by the 7th Lincolns and proceeded to march out to METZ	
LECHELLE	5	12.30	The Battalion marched to LECHELLE and were encamped in huts	
			Orders received for the Battalion to hold itself in readiness to return to the line	
	6		On the M.O.I. (Infantry report the A.D.M.S. held a medical inspection of the men and found that owing to the effects of gas a large majority of Officers and men were unfit for any kind of duty.	
	8		Orders received for the Battalion to proceed to ABBEVILLE area to get ready for Battalion entrainment at YTRES station & for RUE (SOMME) arriving there at 4 am	
RUE	10		on 11th inst.	
	11-31		Battalion resting	
	21		For 3944 Nurses received arrears of pay returning from our bank rolls	

W.W.P.R. Capt

Army Form C. 2118.

WAR DIARY
or
INTELLIGENCE SUMMARY.
(Erase heading not required.)

Original

War Diary
of
2/6th Bn. North Staffs Regiment

from 1st Jany 1918
to 31st Jany 1918

Confidential

Place	Date	Hour	Summary of Events and Information	Remarks and references to Appendices

Instructions regarding War Diaries and Intelligence Summaries are contained in F. S. Regs., Part II. and the Staff Manual respectively. Title pages will be prepared in manuscript.

WAR DIARY or INTELLIGENCE SUMMARY

Army Form C. 2118.

(Erase heading not required.)

Instructions regarding War Diaries and Intelligence Summaries are contained in F. S. Regs., Part II. and the Staff Manual respectively. Title Pages will be prepared in manuscript.

Place	Date	Hour	Summary of Events and Information	Remarks and references to Appendices
RUE	6/11/18		Strength Return 41 960 24 424	X
	11/11/18		Draft of 18 NCOs received	X
	13/11/18		BCM Sgt Dun inspected men who were on the line in the last sessions	X
	13/11/18		65 men to hospital suffering from effects of enemy gas	X
	15/11/18		Draft of 33 OR received from 4th North Staffs Regt	X
	16/11/18		Draft of 11 officers received from 2nd Royal Warwicks Regt	X
	17/11/18		60 other ranks inspected who were on the line on the last session	X
	18/11/18		Draft of 49 OR arrived	X
	19/11/18		92 men to hospital suffering from effects of enemy gas	X
	22/11/18		Bn moved by train to rejoin 59th Div in the LE CAUROY area. Detrained at FREVENT and moved by march route to REBREUVIETTE	M
REBREUVIETTE	28/11/18		Capt H.A.M and 200 OR received from YES Infs Staffs Regt owing to re-organization of Division	M
	29/11/18		Orders received for CO, Adjt and two leading Commanders to reconnoitre the line on the BULLECOURT front or 1st Dec.	M
	30/11/18		No training.	M

R. H. Vann Lt. Col.
Comdg 1/6 N. Staffs Regt

Army Form C. 2118.

WAR DIARY
~~or~~
~~INTELLIGENCE SUMMARY.~~
(Erase heading not required.)

Vol 13

Confidential

Original
War Diary
of
2/6th North Staffs Regiment

From :- 1st Feb. 1915
To :- 28th Feb. 1916

Army Form C. 2118.

WAR DIARY
or
INTELLIGENCE SUMMARY.
(Erase heading not required.)

Instructions regarding War Diaries and Intelligence Summaries are contained in F.S. Regs., Part II. and the Staff Manual respectively. Title pages will be prepared in manuscript.

Place	Date	Hour	Summary of Events and Information	Remarks and references to Appendices
REBREUVIETTE	5/3/18		The Battalion inspected by the M Corps Commander.	M
	7/3/18	10 am	Battalion left REBREUVIETTE by march route to GRAND RULLECOURT arriving there at 1pm.	X
	8/3/18	8 am	March continued to BERLES-AU-BOIS	X
	9/3/18	8 am	Battalion left for HAMELINCOURT (Armagh Camp)	X
	10/3/18	8 am	Battalion left for HAMELINCOURT (Armagh Camp)	X
			Battalion proceeded by bus and march route to relieve the 1/3 (S) Batt East Surrey Regt in the front line (left sub) on Ridge of 1890 - NOREUIL Sector relief complete 10pm.	
NOREUIL	11/12		Situation quiet.	X
			1/4 Coy relief take place every 48 hrs.	X
	14/3/18		Heavy enemy bombardment with 4.2" for looking several hours - casualties W.O. and 5 O.Rs.	X
	15/3/18		Situation quiet.	X
	23/3/18		2% 18th South Staffs Regt relieve the 8th on the night of the 22nd and 23rd. The Battalion moved into the Reserve position at NORY SOUTH CAMP. Relief complete 9 pm.	X
	23.3.18		Battalion found working parties.	X
	24/3/18		Draft of 36 ors arrived.	X
			A & B Coys moved forward to take over the ECOUST-NOREUIL line relieving two Coys of the 5th North Staffs Regt in DEWSBURY TRENCH and IGAREE CORNER	M
	27/3/18		Draft 4.30 ors arrived	M
	28/3/18		Bn relieved the 5th North Staffords in the Right out sector relief complete 9pm	X

273/8

B.M. Moores Lt Col
Comm 14th N. Staffords

59th Division.
176th Infantry Brigade

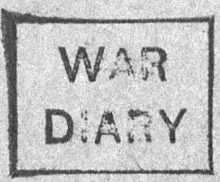

2/6th BATTALION

NORTH STAFFORDSHIRE REGIMENT

MARCH 1 9 1 8

Narrative of Operations attached.

Army Form C. 2118.

WAR DIARY
or
INTELLIGENCE SUMMARY.
(Erase heading not required.)

17b/50 Vol 14

Confidential

Original

War Diary
of

2/6th Bn North Staffs Regiment

From 1st March 1915
to 31st March 1915

Army Form C. 2118.

VOLUME 1 PAGE 1

WAR DIARY
or
INTELLIGENCE SUMMARY.
(Erase heading not required.)

Instructions regarding War Diaries and Intelligence Summaries are contained in F. S. Regs., Part II. and the Staff Manual respectively. Title pages will be prepared in manuscript.

Place	Date March	Hour	Summary of Events and Information	Remarks and references to Appendices
NOREUIL MORY	1	Strength	43 Officers. 963 Other Ranks	
	11	22.00	Battalion relieved in the NOREUIL Sector by 1st Batt. the Hertfordshires and proceeded to SOUTH CAMP MORY on relief.	
	13	3? 00	The Battalion moved from SOUTH CAMP to LE SUCRE (VAUX-VRAUCOURT) to prepare for enemy attack but the attack did not materialise.	
BULLECOURT	19	9.00	The Battalion relieved the 4th Batt. the Kings own Regiment at BULLECOURT west Relief complete 9 p.m.	
	21	6.30	Enemy attack preceded by heavy barrage on the Batt. front. Enemy's advance was well on his right flank of our Cath? "A" Company driven in to Communication and support posn on his right flank of Battalion and reinforcing A.Cos. Bach Coys. All Coy Commanders Casualties. Three Officers Capt PETOREY 2/Lt THORNE 2/Lt LACKS 3 wounded Capt PETOREY 2/Lt ROUSE 2/Lt SLEEMAN S/Lt G. PALMER G.R. ADAMS DEFFRIENS 2/Lt BATCHELOR S.P. HUDSON E.N. UDER Major D/Lt KEATINGE Capt B? CUNYSMITH V.B.C. PALMER G.R. ADAMS DEFFRIENS 2/Lt BATCHELOR S.P. HUDSON E.N. UDER H.R.SMITH & Lts J. PAXTON. P.J. RYAN. A.L. SALTER. T.C. JENNINGS. A.C. IRVINE. B.H. BATCHELOR. 5/4 J.S. COLBOURNE. S.G. POWE. A.T. GREENE. CW FELLOWE ?. W.N.PRICE. R. HEATON. Other Ranks 5/4 2/Lt B. STEARN and 2/Lt V.S. BURTON-SMITH slightly wounded remained at duty Lt C. Bud reported ORLIEUT. H. W. CURTIS D.S.O. 2/6 R.O.H. South Staffs Regt who formed a composite Battalion with to MAJOR H. W. CURTIS D.S.O. 2/6 R.O.H. South Staffs Regt who formed a composite Battalion the battalion Lost 2/Lt R.L. Field at MORY EAST.	
			Lost 2/Lt D.C.B. COTES apparently lost road of Battalion.	
COURCELLES LES COMTE		18.40	O/M. Stan. Bats. Hd. and Transport lines moved by march route to COURCELLES-LES-COMTE.	
DOUCHY	22	1.00	Rest Billets. Battalion (remainder) bus moved by train route to DOUCHY.	
	23	9.30	Orders? Officers evacuated to Hospital. 2/Lt ET. MURPHY evacuated on command of the Battalion.	
BOUZINCOURT BEAUCOURT	25	7.15	The Battalion moved by march route to BOUZINCOURT	
	26	6 am	do BEAUCOURT	
			do FIENVILLERS & CANDAS	

Signatures at bottom

VOLUME 4   PAGE IV
Army Form C. 2118.

WAR DIARY
or
INTELLIGENCE SUMMARY.
(Erase heading not required.)

Place	Date	Hour	Summary of Events and Information	Remarks and references to Appendices
FIENVILLERS – CANDAS	26		2/LIEUT F.A. WILLIAMS 7/6 South Staffs Regt. assumed command vice 2/LT J.MURPHY	
	26	9.00	Old transport moved by marchroute to CAUCOURT via ST POL and LA POUGNAY	
	28	12.45	Battalion less transport moved by train to LA POUGNAY	
LA POUGNAY	29	3.00	Battalion arrived at LA POUGNAY and proceeded by two routes to CAUCOURT where it was joined by the transport	
CAUCOURT	30	11.00	His majesty the King George V	
	30	3.00	Battn. under 2/Lt F.A. Williams was inspected by Major General CERONIER C.B C.M.G. A.D.C. Commanding 59th Division	
			Draft of 120 o/r arrived from Lucknow Wing Reinforcement Camp	

[signatures]

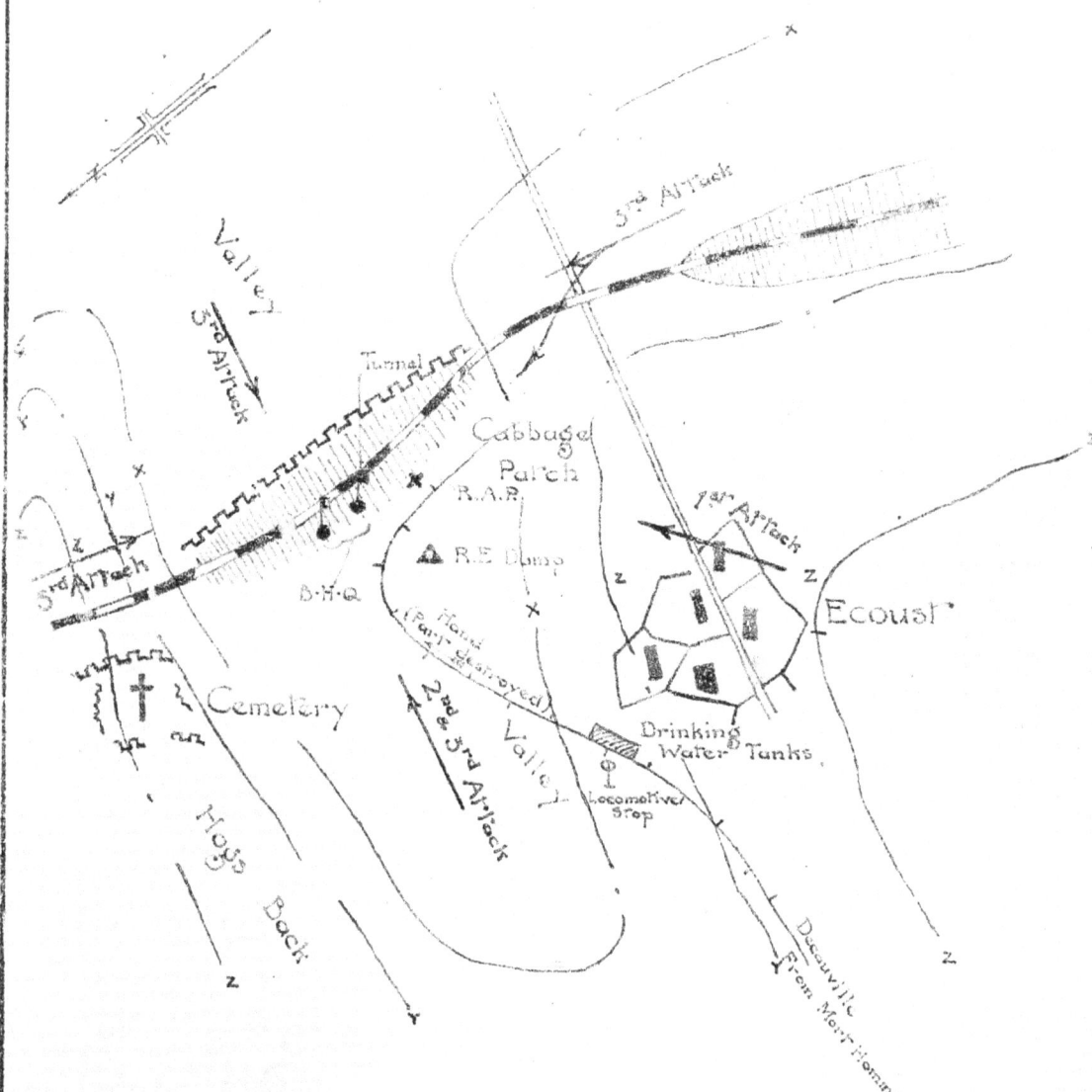

21st March 1918. An Account of Events as
regards 2/6th North Staffordshire Regt.
(Battn Headquarters and A & B Coys) on
that date.

The following facts should be borne in mind throughout the Report:-

(1) On the day in question the weather was naturally misty, and it is reasonable to think that this obscurity was further increased by artificial means.

(2) The Germans had sandbags on their helmets, and, their fighting equipment (packs etc) was so arranged that even at short distances, it was easy to mistake them for our men.

(3) Shortly after the bombardment opened the Bomb Dump was set on fire by direct hit. A large number of "P" bombs burnt for about 2 hours, giving off a dense white smoke, which further increased the obscurity. Also grenades exploding in large numbers rendered it almost impossible to get Lewis gun ammunition and S.A.A. from the Dump close by.

(4) For the first two hours of daylight, it was necessary to wear gas helmets.

(5) Three separate attacks were delivered by the Bosch.

(6) I only came up from Q.M's Base at 8 p.m. the night before, so my remembrance of localities and directions may not be correct.

(7) All telephone communication, except with Brigade Headquarters, which lasted till about 9 a.m. was cut within half an hour of the commencement of the bombardment (4.50 a.m.).

At about 4.50 a.m. I was awakened by a heavy bombardment. The Shell Gas Alarm was sounded. On reaching the top of the embankment I could see that A and B Companies and B.H.Q. were standing to in the proper places in the trench below - I reported to Colonel Thorne.

On the telephone - 6th South Staffords reported heavy bombardment on their whole system, but no signs of attack - 5th North Staffords (Support Coy) reported that they had just been in touch with their B.H.Q. who reported the same - could get no answer to call on 5th North Stafford's B.H.Q. - no answer from E and D Coys (LONGATTE) - Very shortly after this, all telephone communication with front line battalion was cut - buried cable from T.P. at ECOUST to Brigade Headquarters held till about 9 a.m. - Lamps from top of Embankment and Cemetery unsuccessful owing to mist and dust.

Two series of double runners were sent to LONGATTE to receive reports from O's C. C and D. Companies - These never returned.

After about two hours bombardment the barrage on the embankment switched off, but still continued on a general north and south line through ECOUST.

From top of embankment could still not see any signs of attack - saw two Bosch planes working low over our front line - could not hear any rifle or machine gun fire.

About an hour previously an officer's patrol was sent to

left front line battalion (Support Coy). This never returned - subsequently learnt it never reached destination.

Battalion still standing to - hot breakfast was issued.

At about 9 a.m. received a message from T.P. (ECOUST) from Brig.Gen. Cope to the effect that 6th South Staffs reported that enemy had established himself in positions between our forward posts - runner from T.P. reported that they had been ordered to leave their post by B.H.Q. Lieut. Paxton 6th N.S.R. was sent to T.P. with runner and signallers to take over - later Paxton returned to report that he found T.P. vacated and no instrument.

At about 9.50 a.m. saw people moving about in the eastern hedges of ECOUST coming from a southwesterly direction (had previously been in touch with Scottish Fusiliers by runner). These were examined carefully, through glasses, by two or three officers, including myself, who took them for our men.

Five minutes later report was received from right company (B) that they were Bosch - opened fire from Embankment and two platoons were rushed up to Cabbage Patch - Bosch retired - one platoon left in position facing south and on to road running east to BULLECOURT (?)

Meanwhile a wounded Sergeant from the Tyneside Scottish (left Division) came in and reported that Bosch had broken through in large numbers on their front - On this information two platoons were pushed up to hold the high ground round the Cemetery.

At about 11 a.m. saw troops in Artillery formation moving on ECOUST from the direction of MORT HOMME - They looked like our men and were taken to be Reserve Brigade moving into position according to Defence Scheme. Lieut. Stern of the Regiment sent off to the rear with orders to get into touch with Reserve Brigade and act as liaison.

At about 11.30 a.m. fired on heavily from the direction of ECOUST - Platoon on the road was pushed in and reported Bosch attacking in large numbers, and also moving up the road in the direction of ECOUST - also heavy sniping fire from a point on the HOGS BACK about 200 yds west of Cemetery - could still see our men in the trenches round Cemetery firing busily towards the front.

Simultaneously with these events we were attacked by two Bosch planes, flying very low, firing heavy bursts with their M.Gs - although they were heavily engaged no hits observed - These two planes continued to bother us for the remainder of the day.

Bosch troops moving up the road in column towards ECOUST were heavily engaged with L.G. and rifle fire - also an abandoned Vickers gun was brought to bear on them. Severe casualties were inflicted, as I afterwards saw when being taken back a prisoner.

During the last action, our own casualties were heavy. The R.A.P., the tunnel under the embankment, and BHQ were filled with wounded in the space of a few minutes. Our casualties in killed were heavy at all points.

Bosch were again compelled to retire from the eastern edges of ECOUST by our fire from the Embankment - Enemy brought heavy fire to bear, from the ridge running through ECOUST, on

-3-

to the embankment. The embankment was also engaged wide from both flanks with heavy M.G. fire - practically enfiladed.

Time now about 1.30 to 2.0 p.m. - went to report to Col. Thorne on information received from an officer (Lieut. Smith, since died of wounds) to the effect that there did not seem to be many Bosch between us and the Tyneside Scottish, i.e. high ground in front of the Cemetery. My suggestion was to get/into, at least, visual touch with any troops still holding out. As it was both flanks were in danger of being pushed in to the cup formed by the ECOUST valley, which was commanded by high ground on either side. I also still had hopes of Reserve Bde coming up and thought we would be able to hold out longer at Cemetery.

all available men up to this position and by this means get

It took about 20 minutes to work my way back to Col. Thorne - when I reported to him, he said he was certain the Reserve Brigade was coming up - I could still see people moving about on the high ground in rear of ECOUST and near MORT HOMME - nevertheless very heavy rifle fire was still coming from that direction - Col. Thorne advised waiting - I was with the Colonel about half an hour.

While we were still watching, suddenly saw Bosch, in large numbers, moving about ECOUST towards us - An attack was also simultaneously delivered from the road down towards the Cabbage Patch and the dug-out adjoining R.A.P. He obtained possession of the R.A.P. and the dug-out adjoining - He was driven back for a short time, but again obtained possession just after Colonel Thorne was killed - as I was watching over the Colonel's shoulder he received a bullet (explosive) (?) in the head, which killed him instantly.

We were now very much reduced in numbers - about 50 men including wounded, who could still fight - and about 4 or 5 officers, three of whom were wounded including myself.

Made my way back to mouth of tunnel under Embankment. Found trenches and passages blocked with dead and wounded - we were running short of ammunition. Fresh supplies were obtained with great difficulty, as the Bosch had discovered both dumps, and was keeping up a heavy fire on them = men were fighting well - managed to get a few bandoliers off dead and wounded.

Position at the mouth of tunnel gradually became untenable as the Bosch had advanced partly down the Embankment from the south and were firing down into the trenches.

Still thought I could gain high ground round Cemetery - got all available men together and told them to get into tunnel, get into trench on the far side and creep up towards Cemetery till their rear was level with mouth of tunnel and wait for me. Stayed behind and set up a demonstration with two or three men - sent back word to B.H.Q. that anyone there was to come up and join me - waited several minutes but no one came. Afterwards heard from Adjutant that no message ever reached B.H.Q.

Got through tunnel and found Lieut. Cope, who was making bombing blocks, in trench running up to the ECOUST road, bringing fire to bear on the Bosch, who was still advancing down the embankment and trench. Another block was formed at the eastern end of tunnel.

I thought northern end of embankment was still free of

Bosch - Ordered four men to creep up through bushes, get up on top and act as flank guard to my movement towards the Cemetery - These men showed themselves unnecessarily and were immediately killed or wounded - The Bosch then rushed the northern end of Embankment from the western side, obtained possession, and was now firing down on top of us - Just as we were getting to the higher ground, enemy made a rush from the direction of Cemetery and pushed us back - simultaneously he charged the eastern side of the embankment and also broke through the bombing block at tunnel mouth, now in our rear. The Bosch now overlooked us everywhere. We were completely surrounded and captured - in all there were about 12 of us left - time about 4 to 4.30 pm.

During my captivity, I had opportunities of speaking with other officers of the Division, and, I am convinced that we were the last to hold out by two or three hours, at least.

After I was caught, I had an opportunity of seeing the casualties inflicted on the enemy. They were heavy, especially on the road already referred to. These could only have been inflicted by us, as, the guns ceased firing early in the day and the only Vickers guns which spoke were those we brought into action ourselves.

I managed to collect the following information on my way back:- (1) The Bosch advanced up the valleys. (2) They had told their men that they would not find any live British, as the new gas they were using would entirely decimate us - as a matter of fact, this gas was not as bad as that used at BOURLON WOOD - all the way back, I was asked how it was I had managed to survive the gas. (3) A Staff Officer told me that they expected to be in Calais in a week, when the British would be swept into the sea - they had been rehearsing for this since Cambrai - they were very much annoyed when I told them that they had only lengthened the war - they seemed to be anxious about the supposed presence of American troops in our rear. (4) All troops for the attack had been billeted in villages close behind the line - such as VILLERS-CAGNICOURT - for a week before - These villages were not very much damaged by our shell fire. (5) I saw a Bertha firing from a wood just west of ESTREES - I was told it was firing on AMIENS and PARIS. (6) The depth of the attack seemed to stretch as far back as VILLERS CAGNICOURT. (7) Although hit, I could get no anti-tetanus till I reached MARCHIENNES four days later - I was told they had none. (8) If the roads leading through VILLERS CAGNICOURT had been shelled we would have bagged most of their transport - these roads were blocked. (9) They were running up machine guns mounted on bicycle wheels. These went over any ground. (10) I passed through a portion of the ground held by the 6th S.S.R. They must have put up a good fight. The ground was thick with dead, theirs and ours.

I should like to draw attention to the conduct of the following:-

Lieut. Cope, 5th N.S. attached 6th N.S. Acting on his own initiative, this officer organised his position into a defensive post. Under heavy fire of all kinds he maintained his position until ordered to vacate it. He so organised his fire that he inflicted heavy casualties on the enemy.

Lieut. Jennings, L.N.L. attached 6th N.S. The Bomb Dump received a direct hit, which set fire to it. This dump was situated very adjacently to the ammunition dump. Although bombs were exploding in all directions and half choked with fumes from burning "P" bombs, he continued to hand out ammunition for the Lewis guns. He later rendered invaluable assistance by taking charge of a Lewis gun post.

C.S.M. (Acting R.S.M.) Hoeffer, N.Staffs Regt. The conduct of this Warrant Officer throughout the day was beyond praise. He repeatedly organised small posts; saw to the distribution of ammunition and repeatedly took a hand in the fighting. His conduct and demeanour did much to hearten the men and enabled them to hold out for a much longer period than could be thought possible.

Lieut. Paxton, R.Warwickshire Regt. (attached 6th North Staffs Regt.) This officer was one of those sent up to take charge of Cemetery Post. Although badly wounded, he continued to exhort his men, and by his disregard of danger and great courage displayed, held on to his post until entirely overwhelmed. When acting as Signalling Officer, he made repeated attempts under heavy fire of all kinds to patch up the broken airlines.

         (Sd) O.Keating,
           Major,
        2/6th North Staffs Regt.

21st March 1918. An Account of Events as
regards 2/6th North Staffordshire Regt.
(Battn Headquarters and A & B Coys) on
that date.

The following facts should be borne in mind throughout the Report:-

(1) On the day in question the weather was naturally misty, and it is reasonable to think that this obscurity was further increased by artificial means.

(2) The Germans had sandbags on their helmets, and, their fighting equipment (packs etc) was so arranged that even at short distances, it was easy to mistake them for our men.

(3) Shortly after the bombardment opened the Bomb Dump was set on fire by direct hit. A large number of "P" bombs burnt for about 2 hours, giving off a dense white smoke, which further increased the obscurity. Also grenades exploding in large numbers rendered it almost impossible to get Lewis gun ammunition and S.A.A. from the Dump close by.

(4) For the first two hours of daylight, it was necessary to wear gas helmets.

(5) Three separate attacks were delivered by the Bosch.

(6) I only came up from Q.M's Base at 8 p.m. the night before, so my remembrance of localities and directions may not be correct.

(7) All telephone communication, except with Brigade Headquarters, which lasted till about 9 a.m. was cut within half an hour of the commencement of the bombardment (4.50 a.m.).

At about 4.50 a.m. I was awakened by a heavy bombardment. The Shell Gas Alarm was sounded. On reaching the top of the embankment I could see that A and B Companies and B.H.Q. were standing to in the proper places in the trench below - I reported to Colonel Thorne.

On the telephone - 6th South Staffords reported heavy bombardment on their whole system, but no signs of attack - 5th North Staffords (Support Coy) reported that they had just been in touch with their B.H.Q. who reported the same - could get no answer to call on 5th North Stafford's B.H.Q. - no answer from C and D Coys (LONGATTE) - Very shortly after this, all telephone communication with front line battalion was cut - buried cable from T.P. at ECOUST to Brigade Headquarters held till about 9 a.m. - Lamps from top of Embankment and Cemetery unsuccessful owing to mist and dust.

Two series of double runners were sent to LONGATTE to receive reports from O's C. C and D. Companies - These never returned.

After about two hours bombardment the barrage on the embankment switched off, but still continued on a general north and south line through ECOUST.

From top of embankment could still not see any signs of attack - saw two Bosch planes working low over our front line - could not hear any rifle or machine gun fire.

About an hour previously an officer's patrol was sent to

left front line battalion (Support Coy). This never returned - subsequently learnt it never reached destination.

Battalion still standing to - hot breakfast was issued.

At about 9 a.m. received a message from T.P. (ECOUST) from Brig.Gen. Cope to the effect that 6th South Staffs reported that enemy had established himself in positions between our forward posts - runner from T.P. reported that they had been ordered to leave their post by B.H.Q. Lieut. Paxton 6th N.S.R. was sent to T.P. with runner and signallers to take over - later Paxton returned to report that he found T.P. vacated and no instrument.

At about 9.30 a.m. saw people moving about in the eastern hedges of ECOUST coming from a southwesterly direction (had previously been in touch with Scottish Fusiliers by runner). These were examined carefully, through glasses, by two or three officers, including myself, who took them for our men.

Five minutes later report was received from right company (B) that they were Bosch - opened fire from Embankment and two platoons were rushed up to Cabbage Patch - Bosch retired - one platoon left in position facing south and on to road running east to BULLECOURT (?)

Meanwhile a wounded Sergeant from the Tyneside Scottish (left Division) came in and reported that Bosch had broken through in large numbers on their front - On this information two platoons were pushed up to hold the high ground round the Cemetery.

At about 11 a.m. saw troops in Artillery formation moving on ECOUST from the direction of MORT HOMME - They looked like our men and were taken to be Reserve Brigade moving into position according to Defence Scheme. Lieut. Stern of the Regiment sent off to the rear with orders to get into touch with Reserve Brigade and act as liaison.

At about 11.30 a.m. fired on heavily from the direction of ECOUST - Platoon on the road was pushed in and reported Bosch attacking in large numbers, and also moving up the road in the direction of ECOUST - also heavy sniping fire from a point on the HOGS BACK about 200 yds west of Cemetery - could still see our men in the trenches round Cemetery firing busily towards the front.

Simultaneously with these events we were attacked by two Bosch planes, flying very low, firing heavy bursts with their M.Gs - although they were heavily engaged no hits observed - These two planes continued to bother us for the remainder of the day.

Bosch troops moving up the road in column towards ECOUST were heavily engaged with L.G. and rifle fire - also an abandoned Vickers gun was brought to bear on them. Severe casualties were inflicted, as I afterwards saw when being taken back a prisoner.

During the last action, our own casualties were heavy. The R.A.P., the tunnel under the embankment, and BHQ were filled with wounded in the space of a few minutes. Our casualties in killed were heavy at all points.

Bosch were again compelled to retire from the eastern edges of ECOUST by our fire from the Embankment - Enemy brought heavy fire to bear, from the ridge running through ECOUST, on to the embankment. The embankment was also engaged wide from both flanks with heavy M.G. fire - practically enfiladed.

Time now about 1.30 to 2.0 p.m. - went to report to Col. Thorne on information received from an officer (Lieut. Smith, since died of wounds) to the effect that there did not seem to be many Bosch between us and the Tyneside Scottish, i.e. high ground in front of the Cemetery. My suggestion was to get into, at least, visual touch with any troops still holding out. As it was both flanks were in danger of being pushed in to the cup formed by the ECOUST valley, which was commanded by high ground on either side. I also still had hopes of Reserve Bde coming up and thought we would be able to hold out longer at Cemetery.

all available men up to this position & by this means get

It took about 20 minutes to work my way back to Col. Thorne - when I reported to him, he said he was certain the Reserve Brigade was coming up - I could still see people moving about on the high ground in rear of ECOUST and near MORT HOMME - nevertheless very heavy rifle fire was still coming from that direction - Col. Thorne advised waiting - I was with the Colonel about half an hour.

While we were still watching, suddenly saw Bosch, in large numbers, moving about ECOUST towards us - An attack was also simultaneously delivered from the road down towards the Cabbage Patch and the dug-out adjoining R.A.P. He obtained possession of the R.A.P. and the dug-out adjoining - He was driven back for a short time, but again obtained possession just after Colonel Thorne was killed - as I was watching over the Colonel's shoulder he received a bullet (explosive) (?) in the head, which killed him instantly.

We were now very much reduced in numbers - about 30 men including wounded, who could still fight - and about 4 or 5 officers, three of whom were wounded including myself.

Made my way back to mouth of tunnel under Embankment. Found trenches and passages blocked with dead and wounded - we were running short of ammunition. Fresh supplies were obtained with great difficulty, as the Bosch had discovered both dumps, and was keeping up a heavy fire on them = men were fighting well - managed to get a few bandoliers off dead and wounded.

Position at the mouth of tunnel gradually became untenable as the Bosch had advanced partly down the Embankment from the south and were firing down into the trenches.

Still thought I could gain high ground round Cemetery - got all available men together and told them to get into tunnel, get into trench on the far side and creep up towards Cemetery till their rear was level with mouth of tunnel and wait for me. Stayed behind and set up a demonstration with two or three men - sent back word to B.H.Q. that anyone there was to come up and join me - waited several minutes but no one came. Afterwards heard from Adjutant that no message ever reached B.H.Q.

Got through tunnel and found Lieut. Cope, who was making bombing blocks, in trench running up to the ECOUST road, bringing fire to bear on the Bosch, who was still advancing down the embankment and trench. Another block was formed at the eastern end of tunnel.

I thought northern end of embankment was still free of

Bosch - Ordered four men to creep up through bushes, get up on top and act as flank guard to my movement towards the Cemetery - These men showed themselves unnecessarily and were immediately killed or wounded - The Bosch then rushed the northern end of Embankment from the western side, obtained possession, and was now firing down on top of us - Just as we were getting to the higher ground, enemy made a rush from the direction of Cemetery and pushed us back - simultaneously he charged the eastern side of the embankment and also broke through the bombing block at tunnel mouth, now in our rear. The Bosch now overlooked us everywhere. We were completely surrounded and captured - in all there were about 12 of us left - time about 4 to 4.30 pm.

During my captivity, I had opportunities of speaking with other officers of the Division, and, I am convinced that we were the last to hold out by two or three hours, at least.

After I was caught, I had an opportunity of seeing the casualties inflicted on the enemy. They were heavy, especially on the road already referred to. These could only have been inflicted by us, as, the guns ceased firing early in the day and the only Vickers guns which spoke were those we brought into action ourselves.

I managed to collect the following information on my way back:- (1) The Bosch advanced up the valleys. (2) They had told their men that they would not find any live British, as the new gas they were using would entirely decimate us - as a matter of fact, this gas was not as bad as that used at BOURLON WOOD - all the way back, I was asked how it was I had managed to survive the gas. (3) A Staff Officer told me that they expected to be in Calais in a week, when the British would be swept into the sea = they had been rehearsing for this since Cambrai - they were very much annoyed when I told them that they had only lengthened the war - they seemed to be anxious about the supposed presence of American troops in our rear. (4) All troops for the attack had been billeted in villages close behind the line - such as VILLERS-CAGNICOURT - for a week before - These villages were not very much damaged by our shell fire. (5) I saw a Bertha firing from a wood just west of ESTREES - I was told it was firing on AMIENS and PARIS. (6) The depth of the attack seemed to stretch as far back as VILLERS CAGNICOURT. (7) Although hit, I could get no anti-tetanus till I reached MARCHIENNES four days later - I was told they had none. (8) If the roads leading through VILLERS CAGNICOURT had been shelled we would have bagged most of their transport - these roads were blocked. (9) They were running up machine guns mounted on bicycle wheels. These went over any ground. (10) I passed through a portion of the ground held by the 6th S.S.R. They must have put up a good fight. The ground was thick with dead, theirs and ours.

I should like to draw attention to the conduct of the following:-

Lieut. Cope, 5th N.S. attached 6th N.S. Acting on his own initiative, this officer organised his position into a defensive post. Under heavy fire of all kinds he maintained his position until ordered to vacate it. He so organised his fire that he inflicted heavy casualties on the enemy.

Lieut. Jennings, L.N.L. attached 6th N.S. The Bomb Dump received a direct hit, which set fire to it. This dump was situated very adjacently to the ammunition dump. Although bombs were exploding in all directions and half choked with fumes from burning "P" bombs, he continued to hand out ammunition for the Lewis guns. He later rendered invaluable assistance by taking charge of a Lewis gun post.

C.S.M. (Acting R.S.M.) Hoeffer, N.Staffs Regt. The conduct of this Warrant Officer throughout the day was beyond praise. He repeatedly organised small posts; saw to the distribution of ammunition and repeatedly took a hand in the fighting. His conduct and demeanour did much to hearten the men and enabled them to hold out for a much longer period than could be thought possible.

Lieut. Paxton, R.Warwickshire Regt. (attached 6th North Staffs Regt.) This officer was one of those sent up to take charge of Cemetery Post. Although badly wounded, he continued to exhort his men, and by his disregard of danger and great courage displayed, held on to his post until entirely overwhelmed. When acting as Signalling Officer, he made repeated attempts under heavy fire of all kinds to patch up the broken airlines.

                                            (Sd) O.Keating,
                                                    Major,
                                      2/6th North Staffs Regt.

21st March 1918.   An Account of Events as
regards 2/6th North Staffordshire Regiment
(Battn Headquarters and A & B Coys) on
that date.

The following facts should be borne in mind throughout the Report:-

(1)   On the day in question the weather was naturally misty, and it is reasonable to think/that this obscurity was further increased by artificial means.

(2)   The Germans had sandbags on their helmets, and, their fighting equipment (packs etc) was so arranged that even at short distances, it was easy to mistake them for our men).

(3)   Shortly after the bombardment opened the Bomb Dump was set on fire by direct hit.   A large number of "P___" Bombs burnt for about two hours, giving off a dense white smoke, which further increased the obscurity.   Also granades exploding in large numbers rendered it almost impossible to get Lewis Gun Ammunition and S.A.A. from the Dump close by.

(4)   For the first two hours of daylight, it was necessary to wear Gas Helmets.

(5)   Three separate attacks were delivered by the Bosch.

(6)   I only came up from Q. M's Base at 8 p.m. the night before, so my remembrance of localities and directions may not be correct.

(7)   All telephone communication, except with Brigade Headquarters, which lasted till about 9 a.m., was cut within half an hour of the commencement of the bombardment (4-50 a.m.)

At about 4-50 a.m. I was awakened by a heavy bombardment.
The Shell Gas Alarm was sounded.   On reaching the top of the
embankment I could see that A and B Companies and B. Hq. were
standing to in the proper places in the trench below - I
reported to Colonel Thorne.

On the telephone - 6th South Staffords reported heavy
bombardment on their whole system, but no signs of attack -
5th North Staffords (Support Coy) reported that they had just
been in touch with their B. Hq:, who reported the same - could
get no answer to call on 5th North Stafford's B. Hq: - no answer
from C. and D. Coys (LONGATTE) - Very shortly after this, all
telephone communication with front Line Battalions was cut -
buried Cable from T. P., at ECOUST to Brigade Headquarters held
till about 9-50 a.m. - Lamps from top of Embankment and Cemetery
unsuccessful owing to mist and dust.

Two series of double runners were sent to LONGATTE to
receive Reports from O's C, C. and D. Companies - These never
returned.

After about two hours bombardment the barage on the
embankment switched off, but still continued on a general north
and south line through ECOUST.

From top of embankment could still not see any signs of
attack - saw two Bosch Planes working low over our front line -
could not hear any rifle or machine gun fire.

About an hour previously an Officer's Patrol was sent to
left front line Battalion (Support Company).   This never
returned - subsequently learnt it never reached destination.

Battalion still standing to - hot breakfast was issued.

At about 9 a.m., received a message from T.P. (ECOUST)
from Brig-Gen. Cope to the effect that 6th South Staffs reported
that the enemy had established himself in positions between our
forward Posts - Runner from T.P. reported that they had been
ordered to leave their post by B. Hq:.   Lieut: Paxton 6th N.S.R.

was sent to T.P. with Runners and Signallers to take over - later Paxton returned to report that he found T. P. vacated and no instrument.

At about 9-30 a.m. saw people moving about in the eastern hedges of ECOUST coming from a southwesterly direction (had previously been in touch with Scottish Fuslrs by Runner). These were examined carefully, through Glasses, by two or three Officers, including myself, who took them for our men.

Five minutes later report was received from right Company (B) that they were Bosch - Opened fire from Embankment and two Platoons were rushed up to Cabbage Patch - Bosch retired - One Platoon left in position facing South and on to road running east to BULLECOURT (?).

Meanwhile a wounded Sergeant from the Tyneside Scottish (left Division) came in and reported that Bosch had broken through in large numbers on their Front - On this information two Platoons were pushed up to hold the high ground round the Cemetery.

At about 11 a.m. saw Troops in Artillery formation moving on ECOUST from the direction of MORT HOMME - They looked like our men and were taken to be Reserve Brigade moving into position according to Defence scheme. Lieut: Sterm of the Regiment sent off to the rear with orders to get into touch with Reserve Brigade and act as liasion.

At about 11-30 a.m. fired on heavily from the direction of ECOUST - Platoon on the road was pushed in and reported Bosch attacking in large numbers, and also moving up the road in the direction of ECOUST - also heavy sniping fire from a point on the HOGS BACK about 200 yds west of Cemetery - could still see our men in the trenches round Cemetery firing busily towards the front.

Simultaneously with these events we were attacked by Two Bosch Planes, flying very low, firing heavy bursts with their M.G's - although they were heavily engaged no hits observed - These two Planes continued to bother us for the remainder of the day.

Bosch Troops moving up the road in Column towards ECOUST were heavily engaged with L.G. and Rifle fire - also an abandoned Vickers Gun was brought to bear on them. Severe casualties were inflicted, as I afterwards saw when being taken back a prisoner.

During the last action, our own casualties were heavy. The R.A.P., the tunnel under the embankment, and B.Hq: were filled with wounded in the space of a few minutes. Our casualties in killed were heavy at all points.

Bosch were again compelled to retire from the eastern edges of ECOUST by our fire from the Embankment - Enemy brought heavy fire to bear, from the ridge running through ECOUST., on to the embankment. The embankment was also engaged wide from both flanks with heavy M.G. fire - practically enfiladed.

Time now about 1-30 to 2-0 p.m. - went to report to Col. Thorne on information received from an Officer (Lieut: Smith, since died of wounds) to the effect that there did not seem to be many Bosch between us and the Tyneside Scottish. i.e. high ground in front of the Cemetery. My suggestion was to get all available men up to this position and by this means get into, at least, visual touch with any Troops still holding out. As it was both Flanks were in danger of being pushed in to the cup formed by the ECOUST valley, which was commanded by high ground on either side. I also still had hopes of Reserve Bde coming up and thought we would be able to hold out longer at Cemetery.

It took about twenty minutes to work my way back to Colonel Thorne - when I reported to him, he said he was certain the Reserve Brigade was coming up - I could still see people moving about on the high ground in rear of ECOUST and near MORT HOMME - nevertheless very heavy rifle fire was still coming from that direction - Col. Thorne advised waiting - I was with the Colonel about half an hour.

While we were still watching, suddenly saw Bosch, in large numbers, moving about ECOUST towards us - An attack was also simultaneously delivered from the road down towards the Cabbage Patch and the R.A.P. He obtained possession of the R.A.P. and the Dug-Out adjoining - He was driven back for a short time, but again obtained possession just after Colonel Thorne was killed - as I was watching over the Colonel's shoulder he received a bullet (explosive) (?) in the head, which killed him instantly.

We were now very much reduced in numbers - about 30 men including wounded, who could still fight - and about 4 or 5 Officers, three of whom were wounded including myself.

Made my way back to mouth of Tunnel under Embankment. Found Trenches and passages blocked with dead and wounded - we were running short of Ammunition. Fresh supplies were obtained with great difficulty, as the Bosch had discovered both dumps, and was keeping up a heavy fire on them - Men were fighting well - managed to get a few Bandoliers off dead and wounded.

Position at the mouth of Tunnel gradually became untenable as the Bosch had advanced partly down the Embankment from the South and were firing down into the trenches.

Still thought I could gain high ground round Cemetery - got all available men together and told them to get into Tunnel, get into Trench on the far side and creap up towards Cemetery till their rear was level with mouth of tunnel and wait for me. Stayed behind and set up a demonstration with two or three men - sent back word to B. HQ: that anyone there was to come up and join me - waited several minutes but no one came.   Afterwards heard from Adjutant that no message ever reached B.Hq:.

Got through Tunnel and found Lieut: Cope, who was making bombing blocks, in trench running up to the ECOUST road, bringing fire to bear on the Bosch, who was still advancing down the Embankment and Trench.   Another block was formed at the eastern end of Tunnel.

I thought northern end of Embankment was still free of Bosch - Ordered four men to creap up through bushes, get up on top and act as flank guard to my movement towards the Cemetery - These men showed themselves unnecessarily and were immediately killed or wounded - The Bosch then rushed the northern end of Embankment from the western side, obtained possession, and was now firing down on top of us -   Just as we were getting to the higher ground, enemy made a rush from the direction of Cemetery and pushed us back - simultaneously he charged the eastern side of the embankment and also broke through the bombing block at Tunnel mouth, now in our rear.   The Bosch now overlooked us everywhere.   We were completely surrounded and captured - in all there were about 12 of us left - time about 4 to 4-30 p.m.

During my captivity, I had opportunities of speaking with other officers of the Division, and, I am convinced that we were the last to hold out by two or three hours, at least.

After I was caught, I had an opportunity of seeing the casualties inflicted on the enemy.   They were heavy, especially on the road already referred to.   These could only have been inflicted by us, as, the guns ceased firing early in the day, & the only Vickers Guns which spoke were those we brought into action ourselves.

I managed to collect the following information on my way back :- (1) The Bosch advanced up the Valleys. (2) They had told their men that they would not find any live British, as the new Gas they were using would entirely decimate us - as a matter of fact, this gas was not as bad as that used at BOURLON WOOD - all the way back, I was asked how it was I had managed to survive the gas. (3) A Staff Officer told me that they expected to be in Calais in a week, when the British would be swept into the sea - they had been rehearsing for this since Cambrai - they were very much annoyed when I told them that they had only lengthened the War - they seemed to be anxious about the supposed presence of American Troops in our rear. (4) All Troops for the attack had been billetted in Villages close behind the Line - such as Villers - CAGoNICOURT - for a week before - These villages were not very much damaged by our Shell fire. (5) I saw a Bertha firing from a Wood just west of ESTREES - I was told it was firing on AMIENS and PARIS. (6) The depth of the attack seemed to stretch as far back as VILLERS CAGNICOURT . (7) Although hit, I could get no anti-tetanus till I reached MARCHIENNES four days later - I was told they had none. (8) If the roads leading through VILLERS CAGNICOURT had been shelled we would have bagged most of their Transport - these roads were blocked. (9) They were running up Machine Guns mounted on bicycle wheels. These went over any ground. (10) I passed through a portion of the ground held by 6th S.S.R. They must have put up a good fight The ground was thick with dead, theirs and ours.

I should like to draw attention to the conduct of the following :-

Lieut: Cope 5th N.S. attached 6th N.S. Acting on his own initiative, this Officer organised his position into a defens -sive post. Under heavy fire of all kinds he maintained his position until ordered to vacate it. He so organised his fire that he inflicted heavy casualties on the enemy.

Lieut: Jennings, L.N.L., attached 6th N.S., The Bomb Dump received a direct hit, which set fire to it. This Dump was situated very adjacently to the Ammunition Dump. Although Bombs were exploding in all directions and half choked with fumes from burning "P" Bombs, he continued to hand out Ammunition for the Lewis Guns. He later rendered invaluable assistance by taking charge of a Lewis Gun post.

C.S.M., (Acting R.S.M.) Hoeffer, N.Staffs Regt,. The conduct of this Warrant Officer throughout the day was beyond praise. He repeatedly organised small posts. Saw to the distribution of Ammunition and repeatedly took a hand in the fighting. His conduct and demeanour did much to hearten the men and enabled them to hold out for a much longer period than could be thought possible.

Lieut: Paxton, R. Warwickshire Regt, (attached 6th N.Staffs Regt) This Officer was one of those sent up to take charge of Cemetery Post. Although badly wounded, he continued to exhort his men, and by his disregard of danger & great courage displayed, held on to his post until entirely overwhelmed. When acting as Signalling Officer, he made repeated attempts under heavy fire of all kinds to patch up the broken Air Lines.

176th Brigade.

59th Division.

2/6th BATTALION

NORTH STAFFORDSHIRE REGIMENT

APRIL 1918.

Army Form C. 2118.

126/59

WAR DIARY
or
INTELLIGENCE SUMMARY.
(Erase heading not required.)

Original

War Diary
of
2/6th Bn. North Staffs Regiment

From 1st April 1915
To 30th April 1915

Confidential

WAR DIARY
or
INTELLIGENCE SUMMARY.
(Erase heading not required.)

Army Form C. 2118.

VOLUME 4   PAGE 7

Place	Date April	Hour	Summary of Events and Information	Remarks and references to Appendices
CAUCOURT	1	9.00	Strength of Battalion 39 officers 978 other ranks. Battalion proceeded by march route to HOUDAIN where entrained at 3.30pm and detrained at 6.30pm at PROVEN	L/R
PROVEN	2	7.30	Battalion proceeded by march route to St JANS-DER-BIEZEN	L/R
St JANS DER BIEZEN	2		Lieut Colonel J.H. PORTER DSO assumed command of the Battalion	L/R
	3		Draft of 600 ORs arrived	L/R
	4		Battalion reorganised & re-equipped	L/R
		15.30	Battalion inspected by GENERAL SIR HERBERT PLUMER	L/R
	5		Musketry. CLAY PG + NORTH STAFFS RM reported in for course	L/R
	6	16	Battalion march to TRAPPISTES FARM (R17.9 b.5.1) 6 officers & 640 ranks	L/R
TRAPPISTES FARM	7		Battalion march to POPERINGHE	L/R
	8			
	9	10	Battalion arrived by march route to L. Reltinge and detrained at POTIJZE and entrained at POTIJZE	L/R
YPRES	10	9	Battalion relieved EAST SURREY REGT in R. BRANDOEK (G18 & 6.5)	L/R
	11		Battalion in line	L/R
	12	6	Strength of Battalion HANDS	L/R
	12.13		Battalion relieved by 2 East Yorks Regt in R. PASSCHENDAELE sector and proceeded by Lorry to BRANDHOEK. Battalion HQ established at B. Camp 26 a.3.3 (Map sheet 28)	L/R
BRAND HOEK	13	18.30	Battalion proceeded by march route to RENING HEUST. Battalion HQ established at CHIPPEWA CAMP M6a.1.9 (Map sheet 28)	L/R
RENINGHELST	14	3.15	Battalion proceeded by Lorry and transport train to LOCRE. Battalion HQ established at RUDDIGORE FARM N28d.6.5.0.	L/R
LOCRE	15	0.30	Battalion arrived at place 76A2 at BAILLEUL sector. Bn. established at	L/R

J.H. Porter Lt/Col
Cmdg 9th West Yorks Regt

WAR DIARY
or
INTELLIGENCE SUMMARY.
(Erase heading not required.)

VOLUME 4 PAGE 11
Army Form C. 2118.

Place	Date	Hour	Summary of Events and Information	Remarks and references to Appendices
BAILLEUL	15	14.00	Enemy put down a barrage on our trenches and attacked in lines on his first 6 non divisions when the platoons of B Coy under Capt A.J. PAXTON made a bold and gallant attack. Enemy fought severely and eventually retired at & along Railway and forced from the battle to withdraw from the trenches in MONT. d'. LILLE. A counter attack was immediately organised and led by the Commander Other Lieut. Colonel J.H. PORTER DSO and MAJOR WHICLAY MC and Kentucker is estimated at 40 of enemy whilst own casualties were comparatively light. The Battalion was freed to withdraw to the evening slightly through to the left flank and open ground Karo. A but we withdrew to the line Karoo many [illegible] - the right flank by the platoon of C Coy which [illegible] of MG Heavy Grey's weapons to the Holly Crossings Karoo (Sh.28.[illegible]) withdrew as ordered by M. Fire Battalion to Arneguez La Bouhé's Farm at Sh. G 6.7 (Sh.28.[illegible]) withdrew again on the Karoo Brewery Horsha G 3.A 9. [illegible] MAJOR WHICLAY Carried off Lieut R. Ruin Lieut G. MASON Lieut J.H. ROBINSON 2/Lieut A.E. WALKER 2/[illegible] M.C. Capt A.G. PAXTON (2/Lt W.P. SHORT 2/Lt S. OPENSHAW & BEATTY) [Killed] DISMIS[illegible]. 2/LIEUT D. YEAVELDN OPENSHAW 255	JPR JPR
LOCRE	16	9.00	Battalion returned and moved to CLIVER ASH CAMP and settled the accommodation of 14H & 5 [illegible]	JPR
			(Mia Ref. 27)	
	18	13.30	Battalion moved by buses to le TERTINGHER. Halted for 1/2 a cafe until 21.00 a.m (Map Ref[illegible])	JPR
ERQUINGHEM	19	10	Arrived by march route at K.30.c.45 CAMP, PEDELACK 5.25.517E. H.4. K. attained at [illegible]	JPR
			Map Ref. 28	
ERSELINGEN	21	7.15	18th moved by march route to ROUSBRUGGE - HARINGUE AREA on leaving QHK established at	WPR
			B.5. c.6.45. (Map Sheet 27)	
			Coys at H.1.0.A. and 130.0H. arrived	
	24	16.30	Battn. inspected from H.02 18H Reinforcements 3 ORs to be replaced by married I ORs in men for the platoon	JPR
ELLINK	25	18.00	Battn. received reinforcement - 30 ORs DROWN 6.10.6.15 (Map Sheet 27) were in reserve of the Brigade	JPR
	27	16	Battn. less transport moved by march route to take up a line of Redouts locating to C. 30.1480.08	
			HQ established at G.29.d.60.35 (Map Sheet 6.29.4.60.35 as late as 9.25 a 21.27 (Map Sheet 27)	

CONFIDENTIAL

2/6ᵀᴴ N. STAFFS. REGᵀ

WAR DIARY.

for Month of May 1918.

VOLUME III.

Pages 28-32.

Army Form C. 2118.

WAR DIARY
or
INTELLIGENCE SUMMARY.

Volume III
Page 29.

(Erase heading not required.)

Place	Date	Hour	Summary of Events and Information	Remarks and references to Appendices
Ouderdom Switch Line	1		Strength Officers 28 Other Ranks 631	J.F.m
"	2		Draft of 3 Officers (2/Lt W.H. Hurst, 2/Lt A.J. Thomas, 2/Lt F. Kirk) from West Yorks Regt joined the Battalion.	J.F.m
"	5	13.00	Batt: less Transport moved to neighbourhood of TRAPPIST FARM. S.E. of WATOU. Transport and Quartermasters Stores joined the Battalion en route. Batt: H.Q. established at K 16 d. 9. 8. (Sheet 28)	J.F.m Appendix No 1. J.F.m
TRAPPIST FARM	6	14.30	Batt moved by march Route north of WATOU where it embussed and proceeded to the St MOMELIN AREA (N of St OMER) Batt: H.Q. established at KINDERBECK G 26 d 10.05 (Sheet 27)	J.F.m Appendix No 2. J.F.m
KINDERBECK	7		Information received that the Battalion was to be reduced to a Battalion training Cadre as a temporary measure.	J.F.m
	9	11.00	Major General C.F. ROMER. C.B. C.M.G. A.D.C. Cmdg 59 Div presented medal ribbons at a parade of the 176 Inf Bde to the undermentioned officers and men of the 2/6 Bn. N. Staffs Regt for gallantry in action at BULLECOURT on march 21st 1918.	J.F.m
			Lieut-Col W.H.M. Curtis D.S.O (Cmdg 2/6 Batt South Staffs Regt) Bar to D.S.O.	
			2/Lieut A.E. STEARNE M.C.	
			40396 Pte JACKSON L.E. D.C.M.	
			After the presentation of medal Ribbons the Divisional Commander addressed a farewell speech to the Brigade.	

[signature] LIEUT.-COL.
CMDG. 2/6th NORTH STAFFORD REGT.

Army Form C. 2118.

WAR DIARY
or
INTELLIGENCE SUMMARY.

(Erase heading not required.)

Volume III
Page 30.

Place	Date	Hour	Summary of Events and Information	Remarks and references to Appendices
KINDERBECK	9	19.30	Draft of 4 Officers 2/Lt G.V. Woolley, 2/Lt A.S. Marsh. N. Staffs Regt. 2/Lt G.H. Lowry K.O.R.L. Regt. 2/Lt W.H. Kirk, 2/Lt A.J. Thomas, 2/Lt F. Kirk. West Yorks Regt.) and 474 O.R. entrained at ST OMER and proceeded to the Base in order to reduce the Battalion to a Battalion Training Cadre.	1st.m. Appendix No 3 1st.m.
"			4 Officers of the ROYAL WARWICKSHIRE REGT attached to the 2/6 Bn. N. Staffs Regt (2/Lt A. Turner, 2/Lt S. Burton Smith M.M.) 2/Lt L Merriman 2/Lt E.J. Blakemore) proceeded to join their own Regiment.	
"	10	4.45	Batt Training Cadre and Transport proceeded by march Route to MAMETZ arriving at 13.45. Batt Headquarters established at G.35.a.95.30". (Sheet 36c)	1st.m. Appendix No 4 1st.m
MAMETZ	11	7.45	Batt: Training Cadre and Transport proceeded by march Route to FIEFS arriving at 14.30. Batt Headquarters established at A.28.a.6.6. (Sheet 36c)	1st.m. Appendix No 5 1st.m
FIEFS	14	9.45	Batt Training Cadre proceeded by march Route to MAGNICOURT-EN-COMTE arriving at 14.00. Batt H.Q. established at O.35.c.8.0. (Sheet 36c) Batt Transport under 2/Lt A.E. Stearne M.C. remained at FIEFS.	1st.m. Appendix No 6 1st.m
MAGNICOURT-EN-COMTE	16	16.00	Batt Training Cadre moved by march Route to HABACQ arriving at 14.30. Batt H.Q. established at THE CHATEAU HABACQ K&c 15.75 (Sheet 51c)	1st.m. Appendix No 4
FIEFS		9.30	Batt Transport under 2/Lt A.E. Stearne M.C. proceeded to Base for disposal.	1st.m.

[Signed] LIEUT-COL.
OMDG. 2/6th NORTH STAFFORD REGT.

WAR DIARY
or
INTELLIGENCE SUMMARY.

(Erase heading not required.)

Army Form C. 2118.

Volume III
Page 31.

Place	Date	Hour	Summary of Events and Information	Remarks and references to Appendices
HABARCQ	16	17.30	Batt Training Cadre proceeded by march Route to LATTRE ST QUENTIN arriving at 19.00. Batt H.Q. established at J.24.c.15.00. (Sheet 51c.) Lieut-Col J.H. PORTER D.S.O. Comdg 2/6 Batt N. STAFFS REGT. with Training Cadre on his Staff was appointed O.C. Northern Sector of 176 Inf Bde portion of the B.B. Lines. This Batt line was held by 4" Coy Batt R.W.F on the right and 4" Prov Batt Garrison Guards on the left.	1.50 m. Appendix no 8. 1.50 m. 1.50 m.
LATTRE ST- QUENTIN	17	10.00	15 O.R. proceeded to the base for disposal.	1.50 m.
	19	4.45	Batt Training Cadre proceeded by march Route to MAGNICOURT - EN - COMTE arriving at 9.00 Batt H.Q. established at O.34.b.8.2. (Sheet 36f)	1.50 m. Appendix no 9. 1.50 m.
MAGNICOURT-EN -COMTE	20	5.00	Batt Training Cadre proceeded by march Route to LIVOSSART (3 miles N.W. FIEFS) arriving at 10.00. Batt H.Q. established at 6 D.2.4. (Sheet HAZEBROUCK 5A) Information received that the Field Marshall Commanding - in - chief had under authority granted by his majesty the King, awarded the undermentioned decorations for conspicuous gallantry in action at BAILLEUL on April 15" 1918.	Appendix n° 10 1.50 m. 1.50 m.
			Lieut-Col J.H. PORTER D.S.O. (Comdg 2/6 Bn N. STAFFS Regt) Bar to D.S.O	
			2/Lt J. SWALES M.C. Bar to M.C.	
			Lieut (A/Capt) A.G. PATON M.C.	
			240748 Sgt (A/C.S.M) BEE W.A. D.C.M.	

J.H. Porter
LIEUT.-COL.
COMDG. 2/6th NORTH STAFFORD REGT.

WAR DIARY
or
INTELLIGENCE SUMMARY

Army Form C. 2118.

Volume III
Page 32.

Place	Date	Hour	Summary of Events and Information	Remarks and references to Appendices
LIVOSSART	21	5.00	Batt. Training Cadre proceeded by march Route to INGHEM (2 miles N of THEROUANNE) arriving at 10.00	J.T.m
			Batt. H.Q. established at 4.c 85.05 (Sht Hazebrouck 5A).	Appendix No 11 J.T.m
INGHEM	24	9.00	Batt. Training Cadre established a School for the training in Infantry work of the Personnel of 4th Garrison Batts: R.W.K and 4 Provisional Hampshire Garrison Guard Battalion.	J.T.m
"	26		Information received that the training Cadre was to hold itself in readiness to proceed to join 30th Division to assist in training of American Divisions.	J.T.m
"	28	6.00	Batt. Training Cadre proceeded by march Route to WIZERNES where it entrained at 9.00. Train arrived at Pont de Briques East of BOULOGNE at 18.00. T.C.	J.T.m Appendix No 12 J.T.m
PONT DE BRIQUES	29	1.00	Train journey continued. Batt. arrived at NOYELLES-SUR-MER at 8.00 and came under the orders of 66 Div: Batt. for training Cadre proceeded to rest camp at NOYELLES-SUR-MER and continued journey at 12.00 by tractor lorry to CANCHY when Batt. H.Q. were established at 4.K 50.35 (Shut ABBEVILLE 14) Drainage Coy of a Coy under Capt R. Burbage proceeded to DOMVAST. Training Cadre of B Coy under Capt J. Swales M.C. proceeded to FONTAINE-SUR-MER. Training Cadre of C Coy proceeded to St FIRMIN S.W of RUE. under 2Lt C.J. Garrish	J.T.m
CANCHY	30	10.00	Arrival of the Headquarters of the 107 Inf Regt (27 American Division) commanded by Colonel Jennings.	J.T.m
"	31		Strength Officers 8 O.R. 55.	J.T.m

[signature]
LIEUT.-COL.
CMDG. 2/6th NORTH STAFFORD REGT.

Appendix No. 1

SECRET.   OPERATION ORDER NO. 21 A   Copy No. 9.
by
Lieut. Colonel J.H. PORTER, D.S.O.
Cmdg 2/6th North Staffordshire Regiment.

1. MOVE. — The 2/6th North Staffs Regiment will move by march route to Camps in Areas about K.17.a. and E.20.b. central to-day, May 6th.

2. ORDER OF MARCH — H.Qrs. A, B, C, Companies. Companies will move by Platoons at 100 yards interval as far as the junction of the railway and road at G.26.a.5.4. where they will close to Companies and march at 200 yards interval between Companies.

3. ROUTE — Bn.H.Q. — across Country to railway running thorough G.21.c. — thence due west to G.26.a.5.4. thence North to Cross Roads at G.20.a.35;45. — thence West to L.11.a.3.5. — thence West to K.17.a. via road running thorough squares L.10, 9, 8, 7, and K.18 and 17.

4. TIME — "A" Coy. will move off at 1.p.m. and remainder will follow at 100 yards between platoons.

5. DRESS — Overcoats in pack. Ground Sheets to be worn.

6. PETROL TINS — Petrol Tins will be dumped with Lewis Gun Equipment at Bn.H.Qrs.

7. ACKNOWLEDGE.

(Sd) H.T. MORGAN,
Capt & Adjutant,
2/6th North Staffs Regt.

5/5/18.

Distribution —
Copy No. 1   176th Inf. Bde.
        2   C.O.
        3   O.C. A Coy.
        4   O.C. B Coy.
        5   O.C. C Coy.
        6   O.C. H.Q. Coy.
        7   T.O
        8   Q.M.
        9   War Diary
       10   File

SECRET   OPERATION ORDER NO.22 A.   Copy No. 9

by
Lieut Colonel J.H.PORTER, D.S.O.
Cmdg 2/6th North Staffs Regiment.

Appendix No 2.

1. **MOVE.** — The 2/6th North Staffs Regiment will move by Bus and March Route to-day, the 6th instant, to the ST.MOMELIN Area.

2. **BUSSES.** — Busses will accommodate Bn.H.Qrs. "A" Coy. and "B" Coy" "C" Coy. under 2/Lt.C.T.Garrish, will proceed by March Route as per special orders issued to O.C. "C" Coy.

3. **PARADE.** — Bn. will be drawn up in Mass in the centre of the Camp ready to move off at 1.45.p.m.

4. **EMBUSSING.** — Point E.22.d.Central, facing North, on the WATOU – ROUSBRUGGE Road. Head of Column will halt at E.22.d.6.2. on the left of the road, and Companies will close up and be told off in parties of 25 all ranks ready for embussing.

5. **TRANSPORT** — Transport will move to new area under the orders of the Brigade Transport Officer.

6. **DRESS** — Marching Order. Soft Caps will be worn and Steel Helmets carried on the Waterbottle. Box Respirators will not be carried in the "Alert" position.

7. **RATIONS** — Rations for consumption on the 7th will be carried by the parties proceeding by bus, and will be carried on the kitchen by the party proceeding by road. Suitable number of cooking utensils will be carried by each Platoon under Coy. arrangements.

8. **STRENGTH** — O.C. Companies will render to Orderly Room by 11.a.m. a return showing the exact number of Officers and Other Ranks who will be proceeding by bus.

9. **ACKNOWLEDGE.**

                     (Sd) H.T.MORGAN,
                           Capt & Adjutant,
                           2/6th North Staffs Regiment.

Distribution –
- Copy No. 1   176th Inf.Bde.
-           2   C.O.
-           3   O.C. A Coy.
-           4   O.C. B Coy.
-           5   O.C. C.Coy.
-           6   O.C. HQ. Coy.
-           7   T.O.
-           8   Q.M.
-           9   War Diary
-          10   File.

Appendix No. 3.

3.

OPERATION ORDER NO. 30
by
Lieut-Col. J.H. PORTER, D.S.O.

Cmdg 2/6th Bn. North Staffordshire Regiment.
dated 8th May 1918.

Copy No.........

---

1. MOVE. — All Ranks of the 2/6th Bn. North Staffs Regiment who are not retained on the Training Staff will proceed to the Base on the 9th instant.

2. ROUTE. — March Route to Station, ST.OMER.
Train Route from ST.OMER to CALAIS.

3. PARADE. — The Battalion will parade on the field in rear of 'C' Coy. at 2.pm.

4. ORDER OF MARCH — As per margin:-
   Band
   'A' Coy.
   'B' Coy.
   'C' Coy.

5. DRESS. — Full Marching Order. will be
S.D. Caps will be worn and Steel Helmets/carried under Supporting Straps on back of Pack.

6. BAGGAGE. — Officers' Valises and 1 Blanket per man (and rations for consumption on the 10th) will be stacked at the Q.M. Stores at 12 noon.

7. COMMAND. — 2/Lt.G.H.LOWRY will be in charge of 'A' Coy.
2/Lt.G.V.Woolley   do.   do.   'B' Coy.
2/Lt.A.S.Marsh   do.   do.   'C' Coy.
Os.C.Parties will obtain Nominal Rolls, A.Fs.B.122 Movement Orders and other documents from Bn. Orderly Room at 1.30.pm.

8. ENTRAINING OFFICER — 2/Lt.F.E.Burt will report to representative of Brigade H.Q. Staff at 5.15.pm. at the Station, ST.OMER, and take with him entraining state for 2/6th North Staffs Regiment and 3 Companies 5th North Staffs Regiment.

9. INTERVALS. — Intervals of 200 yds between Companies will be maintained on the march.

10. ACKNOWLEDGE.

(Sd) H.T.MORGAN,
Capt & Adjutant,
2/6th North Staffs Regiment.

Distribution -
Copy No. 1 176th Inf. Bde.
         2 C.O.
         3 O.C. 'A' Coy.
         4 O.C. 'B' Coy.
         5 O.C. 'C' Coy.
         6 Q.M.
         7 T.O.
         8 2/Lt.F.E.Burt.
         9 War Diary.
        10 File.

Appendix No 4.

SECRET   OPERATION ORDER NO.31   Copy No......9..
by
Lieut.Colonel J.H.PORTER.D.S.O.
Ref.Maps   Cmdg 2/6th Bn.NORTH STAFFORDSHIRE REGT.
HAZEBROUCK 5A.LENS 11.   dated 9th May 1918.

----

1. MOVE. — The Training Staff and Transport of 2/6th North Staffs Regiment will move by March Route to MAMETZ Sub-area and will continue the march to the TANGRY Sub-area on May 11th.

2. ROUTE. — ST.OMER - BLENDECQUES - HEURINGHEM - ECQUES - REBECQ - MAMETZ.

3. STARTING POINT — Battalion Headquarters.

4. TIME. — Head of Column will pass the Starting Point at 4.45.am.

5. DRESS. — Full Marching Order. Soft Caps will not be worn. Steel Helmets will be carried on the Waterbottle.

6. BAGGAGE. — All Officers Valises, Blankets and Surplus Stores, will be stacked at Q.M.Stores at 4.a.m.

7. ADVANCE PARTY — 2/Lt.F.E.BURT will report to the Staff Captain at the Area Commandant's Office MAMETZ at 10.am to arrange billets.

8. INTERVALS. — Intervals of 20 yards will be maintained between every group of six vehicles.

9. ACKNOWLEDGE.

                                (Sd) H.T.MORGAN.
                                     Capt & Adjutant.
                                 2/6th North Staffs Regiment.

Distribution -
     Copy No.1   176th Inf.Bde.
            2   C.O.
            3   O.C. 'A' Coy.
            4   O.C. 'B' Coy.
            5   O.C. 'C' Coy.
            6   O.C. 'D' Coy.
            7   Quartermaster.
            8   T.O.
            9   War Diary
           10   File.

SECRET   OPERATION ORDER NO.32   Copy No......

by
Lieut.Col.J.H.PORTER, D.S.O.
Cmdg 2/6th NORTH STAFFORDSHIRE REGT.

Ref. Maps Sheet - HAZEBROUCK 5A
Lens 11.   dated 10/5/18.

---

1. MOVE. — The Training Staff and Transport of the 2/6th North Staffs Regiment will move by march route to TANGY Subarea on May 11th 1918.

2. ROUTE — ESTREE BLANCHE - RELY - AUCHY AU BOIS - WESTEREN - FIEFS.

3. STARTING POINT — Cross Roads South of MAMETZ Station.

4. TIME — Head of Column will pass the Starting Point at 7.25.a.m.

5. DRESS — Full Marching Order. S.D.Caps will be worn and Steel Helmets carried on the waterbottle.

6. BAGGAGE — All Officers' Valises, Blankets and Surplus Stores will be stacked at Q.M.Stores at 6.45.a.m.

7. INTERVALS. — Intervals of 30 yards will be maintained between every group of six vehicles.

8. ACKNOWLEDGE.

(Sd) H.T.MORGAN.
Capt & Adjutant.
2/6th North Staffs Regiment.

Distribution -
Copy No.1 176th Infantry Bde.
       2 C.O.
       3 O.C. Company.
       4 Quartermaster.
       5 Transport Officer.
       6 War Diary
       7 File.

Appendix No 6.

SECRET   OPERATION ORDER No.34   Copy No. 8
by
Lieut.Colonel J.H.PORTER, D.S.O.
Cmdg 2/6th North Staffordshire Regiment.

Ref. Sheets - 36 B.
dated 14th May 1918.

1. **MOVE** — The Training Cadre of the 2/6th North Staffs Regiment will move by March Route to-day, 14th May, to MAGNICOURT-en-COMTE.

2. **ROUTE** — FIEFS - SAINS les PERNES - TANGRY - VALRUON - LATEIHULCYE.

3. **STARTING POINT** — FIEFS Church, A.28.a.central (sheet 36B)

4. **TIME** — 9.50.a.m.

5. **DRESS** — Marching Order less Packs. Haversacks will be worn on the back with ground sheets underneath the flap of the haversack. Haversack rations will be carried.

6. **BAGGAGE** — All Officers' Valises, Blankets, Surplus Stores will be stacked at the Bn.H.Qrs. at 8.a.m. One Lorry for Baggage will report at FIEFS Church at 8.a.m. The Q.M. will arrange for a guide to be there to guide this Lorry.

7. **ADVANCE PARTY** — 2/Lieut.F.E.BURT will proceed ahead on a bicycle to meet the Staff Captain at the Area Commandant's Office MAGNICOURT-en-COMTE at 10.30.a.m.

8. **SUPPLIES** — Supplies for consumption on the 15th inst. will be delivered to Units by No.2 Coy. Div.Train.

9. **INTERVALS** — 200 yards will be maintained between Units on the march.

10. **TRANSPORT** — Only Transport allowed for Bn.Training Cadre will be taken. The remaining Bn.Transport under the Bn.Transport Officer will remain at FIEFS.

11. **ACKNOWLEDGE.**

(Sd) H.T.MORGAN.
Capt & Adjutant.
2/6th North Staffs Regt.

Distribution -

Copy No.1   176th Inf.Bde.
       2   C.O.
       3   O.C. Company.
       4   Q.M.
       5   T.O.
       6   R.S.M.
       7   2/Lt.Burt.
       8   War Diary
       9   File.
      10

Appendix No 7.

SECRET.   OPERATION ORDER No.35   Copy No...7...
by
Lieut.Colonel J.H.PORTER, D.S.O.
Cmdg 2/6th NORTH STAFFORDSHIRE REGIMENT.

Refce. Map - LENS 11.   dated 14th May 1918.

1. MOVE.   - The Training Cadre of the 2/6th North Staffs
                      Regiment will move by march route to-morrow,
                      15th instant, to HABACQ, (Sheet LENS 44)

2. ROUTE   - CHELERS - TINQUES - BERLES - HERMAVILLE -
                      HABACQ.

3. STARTING POINT   - Fork Roads at O.35.c.5.1.

4. TIME   - Head of column will pass Starting Point at
                      10.a.m.

5. DRESS   - Marching Order less Packs. Haversacks will
                      be worn on the back with ground sheets under-
                      neath the flap of the haversack. Haversack
                      rations will be carried.

6. BAGGAGE   - All Officers' Valises, Blankets, Packs, and
                      Surplus Stores will be stacked at the Q.M.
                      Stores at 8.a.m.

7. ADVANCE PARTY   - Details will be notified later.

8. INTERVALS   - Intervals of 200 yards will be maintained
                      between Units on the march.

9. ACKNOWLEDGE

                              (Sd) H.T.MORGAN,
                                           Capt & Adjutant,
Issued at 6.pm by Runner.   2/6th North Staffs Regiment.

  Distribution -
              Copy No.1   176th Inf.Bde.
                   2   C.O.
                   3   O.C. Company.
                   4   Q.M.
                   5
                   6   R.S.M.
                   7   War Diary
                   8   File.

SECRET.   Operation Order No. 35a.   Copy No. 7

Appendix No 8.

by
Lieut.Col. J.H.Porter. D.S.O.
Commd. 2/6th. North Staffs. Regiment.

Refce.Map. - 51c.   15th.May.1918.

1. MOVE.   The Training Cadre of the 2/6th. North Staffordshire
                    Regiment will march by March Route xxxxxxxx today
                    the 15th. instant to LATTRE ST.QUENTIN. (Sheet 51c.)

2. ROUTE.   NOYELETTE N Cross Roads at J.23.central - LATTRE
                    ST.QUENTIN.

3. STARTING POINT. Road in front of The Chateau.

4. TIME.   5.30 p.m.

5. DRESS.   Full marching Order and Blankets.

6. BAGGAGE.   All Officers' Valises and surplus stores will be
                    stacked at the Quartermaster's Stores at 5 p.m.

7. ADVANCE PARTY   2/Lt. F.E.Burt will interview the Billet Warden
                    at Lattre St.Quentin at 2.p.m. and will arrange
                    Billets.

8. ACKNOWLEDGE.

                                    (sd) H.T.Morgan,
                                          Captain and Adjutant,
                                      2/6th. North Staffs. Regiment.

Distribution:-

    Copy No. 1. 176th.Inf.Bde.
         2. C.O.
         3. O.C.Company
         4. Q.M.
         5. R.S.M.
         7. War Diary
         8. File.

Appendix W.9.

SECRET   OPERATION ORDER NO.36   Copy No. 9
by
Lieut.Col.J.H.PORTER, D.S.O.
Cmdg 2/6th North Staffs Regiment.

Ref. LENS 11, 1/100,000
    Sheet 51c 1/40,000
    Sheet 36b 1/40,000   dated 18th May 1918.

1. MOVE. — The Training Cadre of the 2/6th North Staffs Regiment will move by march route to-morrow 19th instant, to MAGNICOURT en COMTE.

2. ROUTE — NOYELLE VION - IZEL les HAMEAU - Cross Roads D.7.a.15.90. - TINQUES - CHELERS

3. STARTING POINT — Battalion Headquarters.

4. TIME — 4.30.a.m.

5. BAGGAGE — Officer's Valises, Packs, Blankets, Mess Stores and Surplus Stores will be stacked at the Q.M.Stores at 3.30.a.m.
One Lorry will report at Q.M.Stores at 7.a.m.

6. ADVANCE PARTY — 2nd Lieut.F.E.BURT will report to Area Commandant. MAGNICOURT en COMTE at 7.a.m.

7. HEADQUARTERS — Battalion Headquarters, LATTRE ST QUENTIN will close at 4.30.a.m. and re-open at Billet No.51 MAGNICOURT en COMTE on arrival.

8. ACKNOWLEDGE.

(Sd) H.T.MORGAN.
Capt & Adjutant.
2/6th North Staffs Regiment.

Distribution -
    Copy No.1   176th Inf.Bde.
             2   C.O.
             3   O.C. Coy.
             4   Q.M.
             5   R.S.M.
             6   O.C. 4th P.G.G.Bn.
             7   O.C. 4th Gn.Bn.R.W.F.
             8   File
             9   War Diary.

Appendix No 10

SECRET   OPERATION ORDER NO.37   Copy No...8...
by
Lieut.Colonel J.H.PORTER, D.S.O.
Cmdg 2/6th NORTH STAFFORDSHIRE REGIMENT.

Ref. Maps Sheet - LENS 11, 1/100,000
                  51c, 1/40,000.
                  36b, 1/40,000   dated 19th May 1918.

----

1. MOVE.   - The Training Cadre of the 2/6th North Staffs Regiment will move by march route to-morrow, 20th instant, to PALFART (2 miles N.W. of FIEFS).

2. ROUTE.   - LA THIEUZONE - VALHUON - TANGRY - SAINS les PERNES - FIEFS.

3. STARTING POINT. - Billet No.51.

4. TIME   - 4.45.a.m.

5. BAGGAGE   - Officers' Valises, Packs, Blankets, Mess Stores and surplus stores will be stacked at the Q.M. Stores at 3.30.a.m.
One lorry will report at the Q.M.Stores in the afternoon.

6. ADVANCE PARTY   - 2nd Lieut.F.E.Burt will be at PALFART Church at 9.a.m. to interview the Billet Warden.

7. HEADQUARTERS   - Battalion Headquarters, MAGNICOURT en COMTE, will close at 4.30.a.m. and re-open at PALFART immediately on arrival.

8. ACKNOWLEDGE.

                         (Sd) H.T.MORGAN,
                              Captain & Adjutant.
                              2/6th North Staffs Regiment.

Distribution -

Copy No.	
1	176th Infantry Brigade.
2	Commanding Officer
3	O.C. Company.
4	Q.M.
5	R.S.M.
6	4th P.G.G.Bn.
7	4th G.Bn.R.W.F.
8	War Diary
9	File
10	2nd Lt.Burt.

Appendix No 11

SECRET.   OPERATION ORDER NO. 38   Copy No......

by

Lieut.Col.J.H.PORTER, D.S.O.
Cmdg 2/6th NORTH STAFFORDSHIRE REGIMENT.

Ref. Map Sheet - HAZEBROUCK 5 A.
36 A, 1/40,000   dated 20th May 1918.

---

1. MOVE. — The Training Cadre of the 2/6th North Staffs Regiment will move by march route to-morrow the 21st instant, to THEROUANNE.

2. ROUTE. — LAIERS - CUHEM - ENQUIN les MINES - ENGUINEGATTE.

3. STARTING POINT — Billet No.33.

4. TIME — 4.55.a.m.

5. BAGGAGE. — Officers' Valises, Packs, Blankets, Mess Stores and surplus stores will be stacked at the Q.M. Stores at 3.30.a.m.
Instructions regarding lorries will be issued later.

6. ADVANCE PARTY — 2/Lt.F.E.Burt will be at the Area Commandant or Town Major's Office, BLESSY, at 8.a.m, to arrange billets for the 4th Garr.Bn.R.W.F. He will then proceed to the Area Commandant or Town Major's Office, THEROUANNE at 9.30.a.m to arrange billets for the 4th Prov.Bn.Bn-C.Bn. and this Unit.

7. HEADQUARTERS — Battalion Headquarters will close at PALFART at 4.30.a.m. and re-open at THEROUANNE on arrival.

8. ACKNOWLEDGE.

(Sd) H.T.MORGAN.
Capt & Adjutant.
2/6th North Staffs Regt.

Distribution -
Copy No.1 176th Inf.Bde.
     2 C.O.
     3 O.C Coy.
     4 Q.M.
     5 R.S.M.
     6 4th P.G.G.Bn.
     7 4th G.B.R.W.F.
     8 War Diary
     9 File
    10 2/Lt.F.E.Burt.

Appendix No 12.

SECRET.　　　　　OPERATION ORDER No.39　　Copy No. 8
　　　　　　　　　　　　　by
　　　　　　　　Lieut.Colonel J.H.PORTER, D.S.O.
　　　　　　　　Cmdg 2/6th North Staffordshire Regiment.

Refce. Sheet HAZEBROUCK 5 A.　　　　　　　　dated 27/5/18.

---

1. MOVE　　　　　　　- The 2/6th North Staffs Regt. Training Cadre will proceed to join the 30th Division, and will entrain at WIZERNES Station to-morrow, 28th instant.

2. STARTING POINT　　- Battalion Headquarters.

3. TIME　　　　　　　- 5.45.a.m.

4. BAGGAGE　　　　　- All Officer's Valises, Blankets, Surplus Stores, etc., will be stacked at the Q.M. Stores by 4.45.a.m. Two G.S. Wagons will report to Q.M. to remove baggage, but will not be taken to the new destination.

5. DRESS　　　　　　- Full Marching Order. Steel Helmets will be carried on the back of the Pack underneath the Supporting Straps.

6. RATIONS　　　　　- Rations for the 28th, 29th and 30th instants will be taken.

7. HEADQUARTERS　　- Headquarters will close at INGHEM at 5.45.am. and re-open at new destination on arrival.

8. ACKNOWLEDGE.

　　　　　　　　　　　　(Sd) H.T.MORGAN,
　　　　　　　　　　　　　　Capt & Adjutant,
　　　　　　　　　　　　　　2/6th North Staffs Regiment.

Distribution -
　　　　　　Copy No.1　176th Inf.Bde.
　　　　　　　　　　2　C.O.
　　　　　　　　　　3　O.C. Company.
　　　　　　　　　　4　"A" Mess
　　　　　　　　　　5　Q.M.
　　　　　　　　　　6　R.S.M.
　　　　　　　　　　7　Sergeants' Mess.
　　　　　　　　　　8　War Diary.
　　　　　　　　　　9　File.

ATTACHED 66TH DIVISION

2-6TH BN NTH STAFFS REGT.
JUN 1918 & JULY

ATTACHED 66TH DIVISION

CONFIDENTIAL.

2/6TH N. STAFFS. REGT.

WAR DIARY.

for Month of

JUNE 1918.

VOLUME III.

Pages 33-36

Army Form C. 2118.

WAR DIARY

VOLUME III

Page 33:

(Erase heading not required.)

Place	Date	Hour	Summary of Events and Information	Remarks and references to Appendices
CANCHY	1		Strength - Officers 8, Other Ranks 55:	
	3	8:00	Schools established by Training Cadre at Headquarters of 1st Battn: 108th Infantry Regiment 27th American Division at FROYELLES for the training of Lewis Gunners, Scouts, Musketry Instructors and Physical Training and Bayonet Fighting Instructors:	
			The following Officers, Warrant Officers and N:C:Os; received honours in His Majesty's Birthday Honours published in the Supplement to the London Gazette dated June 3rd 1918.:-	
			DISTINGUISHED SERVICE ORDER.:	
			MAJOR.O:J:T:KEATING:	
			MERITORIOUS SERVICE MEDAL:	
			240846 L/Cpl:R:FODEN) 24222l Pte:G:R:KILLICK)	
			MENTION IN DESPATCHES:	
			Capt:F:E:FOLEY 240672 R:Q:M:S:Scattergood S:J:) 200052 Sgt:R:LECKIE) 10535 Pte:J:FEATHAN)	
	7	14:00	Battn:Training Cadre, less Transport, embussed and proceeded to MONTIERES, arriving at 18:00 and came under the orders of 199th Inf:Bde: Battn:H:Qrs:established at the CHATEAU,MONTIERES, (Map Refce: 1:H:05:55: Sheet DIEPPE 16).- "A" Coy:Training Cadre under Capt:R:BURTON and "D" Company Training Cadre under Capt:T:E:BURT were attached to the 2nd Battn:325th Inf:Regt: 82nd American Division: "B" Coy:Training Cadre under Capt:J:SWALES,M:C: and "C" Coy:Training	

J.H.Poter LIEUT-COL.
C/MDG. 2/6th NORTH STAFFORD REGT.

VOLUME III

Army Form C. 2118.

Page 34

WAR DIARY
or
INTELLIGENCE SUMMARY.

(Erase heading not required.)

Place	Date	Hour	Summary of Events and Information	Remarks and references to Appendices
	8		Cadre under Capt:C:T:GARRISH were attached to 3rd Battn: 325th Inf:Regt: 82nd American Division. Transport, under 2/Lieut:W:WOODWARD proceeded by March Route to MONTIERES, staging for the night at HUPPY:	A.T.W.
MONTIERES	17		Information received that Lieut-Colonel T:B:H:THORNE, who previously commanded this Regiment and who was Missing on March 21st 1918, was to be reported as killed.	A.T.W.
		5:00	Battalion Training Cadre proceeded by march route to MIANNAY. Battn:H:Qrs: established at THE CHATEAU on the West side of the MIANNAY – BOUILLANCOURT Road (Map Refce: 5:I:65:25: Sheet ABBEVILLE 14): The Battalion Training Cadre was attached to the 2nd Battn: 105th Inf:Regt: 27th American Division:	A.T.W.
MIANNAY	19	8:00	Schools established at Headquarters 2nd Battn: 105th Inf:Regt: for the Training of Lewis Gunners, Musketry Instructors, Scouts and Snipers, Physical Training and Bayonet Fighting Instructors: and Signallers of that Battalion:	A.T.W.
		17:00	Battalion Training Cadre proceeded by March Route to BAZINVAL, arriving at 19:30, and came under the orders of 198th Infantry Brigade: Battn:H:Qrs: established at Billet No:14 BAZINVAL (Map Refce: 1:G:85:60: Sheet DIEPPE 16):	A.T.W.
BAZINVAL	20	12:00	Battn:Transport, under 2/Lieut:W:W:OODWARD, proceeded on 3 days march to MOLLIENS AU BOIS (Map Refce: 27:L:65:80:) Sheet AMIENS 17):	A.T.W.

LIEUT.-COL.
2/6th NORTH STAFFORD REGT.

Army Form C. 2118.

WAR DIARY
or
INTELLIGENCE SUMMARY.

(Erase heading not required.)

VOLUME III Page 35

Place	Date	Hour	Summary of Events and Information	Remarks and references to Appendices
BAZINVAL	21	7:00	Battalion Training Cadre proceeded by March Route to GAMACHES, where it embussed on the GAMACHES - EU Road, and proceeded to the III Corps Area.	
PIERREGOT		15:30	Battalion Training Cadre debussed on the PIERREGOT - RUBUMPRE Road and proceeded by March Route to MOLLIENS AU BOIS arriving at 17:00. Battalion Headquarters established at Billet No:7 CAITHNESS Street, MOLLIENS AU BOIS (Map Ref:c: 1.E:65:80: Sheet AMIENS 17). H:Qr:Training Cadre, "B" Coy: Training Cadre, under Capt:J:SWALES,M:C:, and "C" Coy:Training Cadre, under Capt:C:T: GARRISH, attached to 122 M:G:Batt'n: 33rd American Division. "A" Coy:Training Cadre, under Capt: R:BURTON, attached to M:G:Coy: 131 Inf:Regt: 33rd American Division. "D" Coy: Training Cadre, under Capt:T:E:BURT, attached to M:G:Coy: 132 Inf:Regt: 33rd American Division.	
MOLLIENS AU BOIS	23	13:00	66th American Infantry Brigade and 122 American Machine Gun Batt'n: with Training Cadres attached carried out a test manning for 24 hours of the VADEN SWITCH LINE.	
	26	8:45	Battalion Training Cadre proceeded by March Route to PIERREGOT arriving at 9.15 am. Battalion Headquarters established in tents on the PIERREGOT - SEPTONVILLE Road (Map Ref:c: 6.E:50.05: Sheet LENS 11). Battalion Training Cadre attached to 2nd Batt'n: 131 Inf:Regt: 33rd American Division.	
PIERREGOT	27	8:00	Battalion Training Cadre proceeded by March Route to ST:OUEN, arriving at 11:30, and came under	

LIEUT-COL.
O.C. 2/8th NORTH STAFFORD REGT.

WAR DIARY
or
INTELLIGENCE SUMMARY.
(Erase heading not required.)

Army Form C. 2118.

VOLUME III

Page 36

Place	Date	Hour	Summary of Events and Information	Remarks and references to Appendices
ST: OUEN	28	8:00	the orders of 199 Infantry Brigade. Battn:H:Qrs: established at Billet No:2 Rue d'AMIENS (Map Refce: 6:B:50:45 Sheet LENS 11): Battalion Training Cadre proceeded by March Route to YAUCOURT-BUSSES arriving at 10:30. Battn: Headquarters established at THE CHATEAU, YAUCOURT-BUSSUS (Map Refce: 5:L:80:25: Map Sheet ABBEVILLE 14): Battalion Training Cadre attached to 2nd Battn: 129 Inf:Regt: 33rd American Division:	
YAUCOURT-BUSSUS.	30		Strength - 8 Officers 52 O.Rs.	

[signature]
LIEUT.-COL.
CMDG. 2/6th NORTH STAFFORD REGT.

WAR DIARY

VOLUME III — Army Form C. 2118.

Page 33:

(Erase heading not required.)

Place	Date	Hour	Summary of Events and Information	Remarks and references to Appendices
CANCHY	1		Strength – Officers 8, Other Ranks 55:	
	3	8:00	Schools established by Training Cadre at Headquarters of 1st Battn: 108th Infantry Regiment 27th American Division at FROYELLES for the training of Lewis Gunners, Scouts, Musketry Instructors and Physical Training and Bayonet Fighting Instructors:	
			The following Officers, Warrant Officers and N.C.O(s): received honours in His Majesty's Birthday Honours published in the supplement to the London Gazette dated June 3rd 1918:-	
			DISTINGUISHED SERVICE ORDER:-	
			MAJOR. C:J:F:KEATING	
			MERITORIOUS SERVICE MEDAL:	
			240846 L/Cpl:R:TUDEN) 242221 Pte:C:R:KILLICK)	
			MENTION IN DESPATCHES:	
			Capt:F:E:FOLEY 24672 R:Q:M:S:Scattergood S:J:) 20052 Sgt:R:LECKIE) 10535 Pte:J:PEATMAN)	
	7	14:00	Battn:Training Cadre, less Transport, embussed and proceeded to MONTIERES, arriving at 18:00 and came under the orders of 199th Inf:Bde: Battn:H:Qrs:established at the CHATEAU,MONTIERES, (Map Refce: 1:H:(5.55: Sheet DIEPPE 16): "A" Coy:Training Cadre under Capt:R:BURTON and "D" Company Training Cadre under Capt:F:E:BURT were attached to the 2nd Battn:325th Inf:Regt: 82nd American Division: "B" Coy:Training Cadre under Capt:J:SWALES,M:C: and "C" Coy:Training	Appendix No.1.

L.H. Porter, LIEUT.-COL.
C.O. 2/6th NORTH STAFFORD REGT.

Army Form C. 2118.

WAR DIARY
or
INTELLIGENCE SUMMARY.
(Erase heading not required.)

VOLUME III
Page 34

Place	Date	Hour	Summary of Events and Information	Remarks and references to Appendices
			Cadre under Capt:C:T:GARDISH were attached to 3rd Battn: 325th Inf:Regt: 82nd American Division: Transport, under 2/Lieut:W:WOODWARD proceeded by March Route to MONTIERES, staging for the night at HUPPY:	Appendix No 2
MONTIERES	8		Information received that Lieut-Colonel T:B:H:THORNE, who previously commanded this Regiment and who was missing on March 21st 1918, was to be reported as killed:	
	17	5:00	Battalion Training Cadre proceeded by march route to MIANNAY, arriving at 10:45: and came under the orders of 197th Infantry Regiment: Battn:H:Qrs: established at THE CHATEAU on the West side of the MIANNAY - BOUILLANCOURT Road (Map Refce: 5:I:65:25: Sheet ABBEVILLE 14): The Battalion Training Cadre was attached to the 2nd Battn: 105th Inf:Regt: 27th American Division:	Appendix No.3
MIANNAY	19	8:00	Schools established at Headquarters 2nd Battn: 105th Inf:Regt: for the training of Lewis Gunners, Musketry Instructors, Scouts and Snipers, Physical Training and Bayonet Fighting Instructors: and Signallers of that Battalion:	
		17:00	Battalion Training Cadre proceeded by March Route to BAZINVAL, arriving at 19:30, and came under the orders of 198th Infantry Brigade: Battn:H:Qrs: established at Billet No.14 BAZINVAL (Map Refce: 1:G:85:60: Sheet DIEPPE 16):	Appendix No.4
BAZINVAL	20	12:00	Battn:Transport, under 2/Lieut:W:WOODWARD, proceeded on 3 days march to MOLLIENS AU BOIS (Map Refce: (A27:E:65:80:) Sheet AMIENS 17):	Appendix No.5

LIEUT.-COL.
O/dg. 2/8th NORTH STAFFORD REGT.

Army Form C. 2118.

WAR DIARY or INTELLIGENCE SUMMARY.

(Erase heading not required.)

VOLUME III   Page 35

Instructions regarding War Diaries and Intelligence Summaries are contained in F.S. Regs., Part II. and the Staff Manual respectively. Title pages will be prepared in manuscript.

Place	Date	Hour	Summary of Events and Information	Remarks and references to Appendices
BAZINVAL	21	7:00	Battalion Training Cadre proceeded by March Route to GAMACHES, where it embussed on the GAMACHES - EU Road, and proceeded to the III Corps Area.	Appendix No.6
PIERREGOT		15:30	Battalion Training Cadre debussed on the PIERREGOT - RUBUMPRE Road and proceeded by March Route to MOLLIENS AU BOIS arriving at 17:00. Battalion Headquarters established at Billet No.7 CAITNESS Street, MOLLIENS AU BOIS (Map Refce. 1:B:65:80: Sheet AMIENS 17): H.Q:.Training Cadre, "B" Coy. Training Cadre, under Capt:J:SWALES,M:C., and "C" Coy.Training Cadre, under Capt:C.T. GARRISH, attached to 122 M:G:Batta: 33rd American Division. "A" Coy.Training Cadre, under Capt: R.BURTON, attached to M:G:Coy: 131 Inf:Regt: 33rd American Division. "D" Coy: Training Cadre, under Capt:T:E:BURT, attached to M:G:Coy: 132 Inf:Regt: 33rd American Division:	
MOLLIENS AU BOIS	23	13:00	66th American Infantry Brigade and 122 American Machine Gun Battn: with Training Cadres attached carried out a test manning for 24 hours of the VADEN SWITCH LINE:	
	26	8:45	Battalion Training Cadre proceeded by March Route to PIERREGOT arriving at 9:15 am: Battalion Headquarters established in tents on the PIERREGOT – SEPTENVILLE Road (Map Refce: 6:B:50:05: Sheet LENS 11). Battalion Training Cadre attached to 2nd Battn: 131 Inf:Regt: 33rd American Division:	Appendix No.7
PIERREGOT	27	8:00	Battalion Training Cadre proceeded by March Route to ST:OUEN, arriving at 11:30. and came under	Appendix No.8

J.H. ??? LIEUT:COL.
CMDG. 2/6th NORTH STAFFORD REGT.

WAR DIARY
or
INTELLIGENCE SUMMARY.

(Erase heading not required.)

Army Form C. 2118.

VOLUME III   Page 36

Place	Date	Hour	Summary of Events and Information	Remarks and references to Appendices
ST: OUEN	28	8:00	the orders of 199 Infantry Brigade. Battn:H:Qrs: established at Billet No:2 Rue d'AMIENS (Map Ref:ce: 6:B:50:45 Sheet 'ENS 11).	Battn: Appendix No 9
			Battalion Training Cadre proceeded by March Route to YAUCOURT-BUSSES arriving at 10:30.	ditto
			Headquarters established at THE CHATEAU, YAUCOURT-BUSSUS (Map Ref:ce: 5:L:80:25: Map Sheet ABBEVILLE 14): Battalion Training Cadre attached to 2nd Battn: 129 Inf:Regt: 33rd American Division:	ditto
YAUCOURT-BUSSUS	30		Strength - 8 Officers 52 O.Rs.	

[signature]
LIEUT.-COL.
COMDG. 2/6th NORTH STAFFORD REGT.

CONFIDENTIAL.

2/6TH NORTH STAFFS. REGT.

WAR DIARY.

for Month of

JULY 1918.

Volume III

Pages 37 & 38.

CONFIDENTIAL

2/6TH NORTH. STAFFS. REGT.

WAR DIARY

for Month of

JULY 1918

VOLUME III.

Pages 37 & 38.

Army Form C. 2118.

WAR DIARY
or
INTELLIGENCE SUMMARY.

VOLUME 3 Page 37:

(Erase heading not required.)

Instructions regarding War Diaries and Intelligence Summaries are contained in F. S. Regs., Part II. and the Staff Manual respectively. Title pages will be prepared in manuscript.

Place	Date	Hour	Summary of Events and Information	Remarks and references to Appendices
YAUCOURT-BUSSUS:	1		Strength - Officers 8 Other Ranks 52:	J.T.m.
	3	6:45	Battalion Training Cadre proceeded by March Route to DOULLENS, staging for the night of 3/4th July at BERNAVILLE which was reached at 11:00: Battalion Headquarters established at billet No:41 A BERNAVILLE (Map Ref: 5:C:05:65 Map Sheet LENS 11)	J.T.m.
BERNAVILLE	4	6:45	Battalion Training Cadre continued march to DOULLENS and arrived at 10:00 Battn:H:Qrs: established at Billet No:H7 Place EUGENE ANDRIEU, DOULLENS. (Map Ref: 5:E:05:90: Sheet LENS 11) Battalion Training Cadre came under "Composite Brigade 66th Division, Commanded by Lieut:Col: M:P:HANCOCK, D:S:O:., and was attached to 317th Infantry Regiment 80th American Division:	J.T.m.
DOULLENS	6	3:00	Arrival of 317th Infantry Regiment, 80th American Division, commanded by Col:PERRY: "A" Company Training Cadre under Capt:R:BURTON, and "D" Coy: Training Cadre under Capt:F:E:BURT, and "C" Company Training Cadre 2/5th Manchester Regiment, attached to 1st Battalion 317th Infantry Regt: "B" Company Training Cadre under Capt:J:SWALES, M:C: and"C" Coy:Training Cadre under Capt:C:T: GARRISH, attached to 2nd Battn: 317th Infantry Regt: 3 Coy:Training Cadres of 2/5th Manchester Regt: under Capt:R:ELLIS and Capt:J:THOMPSON were attached to 3rd Battn: 317th Infantry Regt:	J.T.m.
	22	12:45	Battalion Training Cadre moved by March Route to CANDAS and entrained there at 3:pm: for SERQUEX (Map Ref: 5 G Central, Map Sheet DIEPPE 16) arriving at 22:30:	J.T.m.

Army Form C. 2118.

WAR DIARY
or
INTELLIGENCE SUMMARY.
(Erase heading not required.)

Instructions regarding War Diaries and Intelligence Summaries are contained in F. S. Regs., Part II. and the Staff Manual respectively. Title pages will be prepared in manuscript.

Place	Date	Hour	Summary of Events and Information	Remarks and references to Appendices
SERQUEX	23	1:00	Training Cadre proceeded by March Route to ABANCOURT AREA arriving at 2:30; Headquarters established immediately North of E in HULEUX, 4 I:6:4 (Map DIEPPE 16) Training Cadre came under orders of 198th Infantry Brigade; Information received that 2/6th North Staffs Regt. is to be disbanded:	J.T.M.
ABANCOURT AREA	26 30-79 31 /45.		Training Cadre, less transport, proceeded by March Route to ROMESCAMPS where it entrained for 1/6th Battn. North Staffordshire Regiment. Transport proceeded by March Route to Advanced Horse Depot, ABBEVILLE:	J.T.M.
			Battalion disbanded.	J.T.M.

J. H. Foster
LIEUT. COL.
CMDG. 2/6th NORTH STAFFORD REGT.

Army Form C. 2118.

WAR DIARY
or
INTELLIGENCE SUMMARY.
(Erase heading not required.)

VOLUME 3   Page 37.

Place	Date	Hour	Summary of Events and Information	Remarks and references to Appendices
VAUCOURT	1		Strength – Officers 8 Other Ranks 52.	
BUSSUS:	3	6:45	Battalion Training Cadre proceeded by March Route to DOULLENS, staging for the night of 3/4th July at BERNAVILLE which was reached at 11:00. Battalion Headquarters established at Billet No.41 A BERNAVILLE (Map Ref: 5:0:05:65 Map Sheet LENS 11)	Appendix 1
BERNAVILLE	4	6:45	Battalion training Cadre continued march to DOULLENS and arrived at 10:00. Battn:H.Qrs: established at Billet No:H7 Place EUGENE ANDRIEU, DOULLENS. (Map Ref: 5:B:05:90: Sheet LENS 11) Battalion Training Cadre came under Composite Brigade 66th Division, Commanded by Lieut:Col: M:P:HANCOCK, D:S:O:, and was attached to 317th Infantry Regiment 80th American Division.	Appendix 2
DOULLENS	6	3:00	Arrival of 317th Infantry Regiment, 80th American Division, commanded by Col:PERRY: "A" Company Training Cadre under Capt.R:BURTON, and "D" Coy: Training Cadre under Capt:P:B:BURT, and "C" Company Training Cadre 2/5th Manchester Regiment, attached to 1st Battalion 317th Infantry Regt. "B" Company Training Cadre under Capt:J:SWALES, M:C: and "C" Coy: Training Cadre under Capt:C:T: GARRISH, attached to 2nd Battn: 317th Infantry Regt. 3 Coy: Training Cadres of 2/5th Manchester Regt: under Capt:R:ELLIS and Capt:J:THOMPSON were attached to 3rd Battn: 317th Infantry Regt.	
	22	12:45	Battalion Training Cadre moved by March Route to CANDAS and entrained there at 3:pm: for SERQUEX (Map Ref: 5 G Central, Map Sheet DIEPPE 16) arriving at 22:30.	Appendix 3

[signature] LIEUT.-COL.
CMDG. 2/6th NORTH STAFFORD REGT.

WAR DIARY
or
INTELLIGENCE SUMMARY.
(Erase heading not required.)

Army Form C. 2118.

Place	Date	Hour	Summary of Events and Information	Remarks and references to Appendices
SERQUEX	23	1.00	Training Cadre proceeded by March Route to ABANCOURT AREA arriving at 2:30: Headquarters established immediately North of E in HUEUX, 4 I:6:4 (Map DIEPPE 16) Training Cadre came under orders of 198th Infantry Brigade: Information received that 2/6th North Staffs Regt: is to be disbanded.	
ABANCOURT AREA	31	7.45	Training Cadre, less transport, proceeded by March Route to ROMESCAMPS where it entrained for 1/6th Battn. North Staffordshire Regt. Transport proceeded by March Route to Advanced Horse Depot, ABBEVILLE: Battalion disbanded.	Appendix 4

signature
LIEUT-COL
CMDG. 2/6th NORTH STAFFORD REGT.

Appendix No 1

SECRET.   OPERATION ORDER No. 49   Copy No...9...
                              by
                   Lieut Colonel J.H.PORTER, D.S.O.
                   Cmdg 2/6th North Staffordshire Regiment.

Refce Map ABBEVILLE 1/100,000.   a/a 7th June 1918.
━━

1. MOVE.   — The Training Cadre 2/6th North Staffs Regiment
                      will be relieved by H.Qrs. and 3 Coys. 6th Lancs.
                      Fusiliers, and 1 Coy. 2/7th Lancs Fusiliers, in
                      CRECY Sub-area on Friday, June 7th, and will
                      proceed by Lorry to MONTIERES (less two Companies
                      in tents on the MONTIERES-GAMACHES Road), for
                      attachment to the 2nd and 3rd Battalions, 325
                      Infantry Regiment.

2. O.C. Training Cadre at FROYELLES and O.C. Training Cadre at DOMVAST
   will arrange to report at these Headquarters by
   12 noon on the 7th instant, with their Training
   Cadre and Instructors attached.

3. TRAINING.   — In order to ensure continuity of work O.C. Coy.
                      Training Cadres will hand over all programmes of
                      work and information about their areas to
                      incoming Cadres, and at the same time obtain as
                      much information as possible about the areas they
                      are taking over.

4. The Quartermaster will arrange for the G.S Wagon to report to O.C.
   "A" Coy. Training Cadre at DOMVAST and "B" Coy.
   at FROYELLES in order to collect Baggage.
   An extra baggage wagon has been detailed by the
   66th Divisional Train to report to this Unit.

5. BAGGAGE.   — All Officers' Valises, Blankets (rolled in bundles
                      of ten), and surplus stores will be stacked at the
                      Q.M. Stores by 11.a.m.

6. DRESS   — All Other Ranks will wear Full Marching Order.

7. HEADQUARTERS   — Headquarters will close at CANCHY at 1.p.m. and
                      re-open at MONTIERES on arrival.

8. ACKNOWLEDGE.

                                   (Sd) H.T.MORGAN,
                                          Capt & Adjutant,
Issue by S.D.R. at   4.a.m.   2/6th North Staffs Regiment.

           Distribution.—
                    Copy No.1   199th Inf.Bde.
                         2   C.O.
                         3   O.C. "A" Coy.
                         4   O.C. "B" Coy.
                         5   O.C. "C" Coy.
                         6   O.C. "D" Coy.
                         7   Q.M.
                         8   R.S.M.
                         9   War Diary.
                        10   File.

Appendix No.2.

SECRET.   OPERATION ORDER No. 40A   Copy No. 9
by
Lieut Colonel J.H. PORTER, D.S.O.
Cmdg 2/6th North Staffordshire Regiment.

Refce. Maps - ABBEVILLE 14, 1/100,000.
        DIEPPE   16, 1/100,000.   a/a 7/6/18.

----

1. — Reference Operation Order No. 40 issued to-day, the Transport of the Training Cadre of this Battalion under 2nd Lieut. W. Woodward will proceed by road to MONTIERES, (Map DIEPPE 16, 1/100,000; 1 H. 45. 65.)) S.E. of GAMACHES.

2. ROUTE — ABBEVILLE - ST. MARGUERITE - VILLERS-sur-MAREUIL - ST. MAXENT-en-VIMEU - TRANSLAY - BOUTTENCOURT - MONTIERS.

3. STARTING POINT — Battalion Headquarters.

4. TIME —

5. TRAFFIC — Attention is called to Army Routine Order No. 2039, dated 15th May 1918, "Traffic Rules", issued to all Officers on 4/6/18.

6. ACKNOWLEDGE.

                    (Sd) H.T. MORGAN,
                         Capt & Adjutant.
Issued by S.D.R. at 12 noon.   2/6th North Staffs Regiment.

        Distribution:-
            Copy No. 1 198th Inf. Bde.
                     2 C.O.
                     3 O.C. "A" Coy.
                     4 O.C. "B" Coy.
                     5 O.C. "C" Coy.
                     6 O.C. "D" Coy.
                     7 Q.M.
                     8 R.S.M.
                     9 War Diary
                    10 File
                    11 2nd Lieut. W. Woodward.

SECRET. Appendix No.   OPERATION ORDER No. 44.   Copy No. 7
                         by
                    Lieut. Colonel J.K.PORTER. D.S.O.
                    Cmdg 2/6th North Staffordshire Regiment.

Refce Maps ABBEVILLE 44, 1/100,000.
           DIEPPE 26, 1/100,000.   dated 16/6/18.

----

1. MOVE.   - The Training Cadre, 2/6th North Staffs Regiment,
                      will move to-morrow, 17th instant, by march route
                      to MIANNAY (Sheet ABBEVILLE 44, O.1.60.87) and
                      will be attached to "B" Battn. 168th American
                      Infantry Regiment.

2. ROUTE.   - (i) PERSONNEL.
                      MONTIERES - BOUILLANCOURT-en-SERY - INFRAY -
                      MAISNEVILLE - FRETTEMEULE - COURTIEUX - TOEUFLES -
                      MIANNAY.
                      (ii) TRANSPORT.
                      MONTIERES - GAMACHES - MAISINIERES - TOEUFLES -
                      MIANNAY.

3. STARTING POINT   - On road outside Chateau (Bn.H.Qrs.).

4. TIME.   - 5.a.m.

5. BAGGAGE   - All Officers' Valises, Blankets rolled in bundles
                      of ten, and surplus stores will be stacked at
                      the Q.M. Stores by 4.a.m.

6. DRESS.   - All Other Ranks will wear full marching order.

7. TRANSPORT   - The Transport will proceed under the command of
                      2nd Lieut.W.Woodward. Bicycles will proceed with
                      the personnel.

8. BILLETING   - Capt.F.E.Dust will proceed ahead and find out
                      accommodation for the Battalion.

9. TRAINING CADRES - Os.C. "B" & "C" Coy. Training Cadres will move to
                      MONTIERES to-night after handing over Camp and
                      all Stores to representative of 2nd Bn. 166th
                      American Infantry Regiment.
                      Os.C. "A" & "D" Coy. Training Cadres will hand
                      over tents, camp equipment etc. to 3rd Bn.166th
                      American Infantry Regiment.
                      Receipts will be obtained in both cases and
                      handed in to the Orderly Room.
                      DIEPPE Maps and all Maps of Training Area will be
                      handed in to XxxXxXxx Orderly Room to-night.

10. HEADQUARTERS.   - Headquarters will close at MONTIERES at 5.a.m. and
                      re-open at MIANNAY on arrival.

11. ACKNOWLEDGE.

                            (Sd). D.T.MORGAN,   Capt & Adjutant.
                                                2/6th North Staffs Regiment.

        Copy No.1   199 Inf.Bde.
             2   C.O.
             3   O.C. "A" Coy.
             4   O.C. "B" Coy.
             5   O.C. "C" Coy.
             6   O.C. "D" Coy.
             7   Q.M.
             8   R.S.M.
             9   War Diary.
            10   File.

Appendix No.

SECRET.   OPERATION ORDER No. 42   Copy No. 9.
by
Lieut. Colonel J.K.PORTER. D.S.O.
C-dg 2/6th North Staffordshire Regiment.

Refce Maps ABBEVILLE 14, 1/200,000
DIEPPE 10, 1/200,000.   dated 15/6/18.

----

1. MOVE. — The 2/6th North Staffs Regiment Training Cadre will move by March Route on June 18th to BAZINVAL.

2. ROUTE. — MIANAY - BOUILLANCOURT - TOEUFLES - TOURS-en-VIMEU - MAISINIERES - GAMACHES - BAZINVAL.

3. STARTING POINT — Battalion Headquarters.

4. TIME — 4.p.m.

5. DRESS — Full Marching Order.

6. BAGGAGE — All Officers' Valises, Blankets, surplus stores, etc. will be stacked at the Q.M. Stores immediately

7. ACKNOWLEDGE.

(Sd) H.T.MORGAN,
Captn & Adjutant.
2/6th North Staffs Regiment.

Distribution -
Copy No. 1   197 Inf Bde.
         2   C.O.
       3-6   O.C. Companies.
         7   Q.M.
         8   R.S.M.
         9   War Diary
        10   File.

appendix No. 5.

SECRET   OPERATION ORDER No. 42   Copy No. 5
                    by
          Lieut.Colonel J.H.PORTER, D.S.O.
          Cmdg 2/6th North Staffordshire Regiment.

Refce Sheets AMIENS 17, 1/250,000
             DIEPPE 16, 1/100,000
             ABBEVILLE, 14, 1/100,000
             LENS 11, 1/100,000.   26th June 1918.

1. MOVE.   - The Transport of the 2/6th North Staffs Training
                    Cadre will move by march route with Transport of
                    the 3rd Bn. 132nd Infantry Regiment, 33rd American
                    Division, on June 20th, 21st and 22nd 1918, in
                    accordance with attached march table.

2. COMMAND.   - The Transport will be under the command of 2nd Lt.
                    W.Woodward, who will leave these Headquarters at
                    11.45.a.m. on June 20th in order to reach the
                    Starting Point laid down by the 66th Division at
                    1.p.m.

3. ACKNOWLEDGE.

                              (Sd) H.T.MORGAN,
                                         Capt & Adjutant.
                                         2/6th North Staffs Regiment.

     Distribution -
       Copy No. 1 C.O.
                2 2/Lt. W.WOODWARD.
                3 Q.M.
                4 File
                5 War Diary.

     MARCH TABLE TO ACCOMPANY 2/6th North Staffs Operation Order No. 42.

Date.	British Unit	Aff.American Unit.	From	To.
20th	2/6th N.Staffs.	3/132 Battn.	GAMACHES Area	HARTAIN-NEVILLE Area
21st			HARTAIN-NEVILLE Area.	LONG Area (BRUCAMP & AILLY Sub-Area)
22nd			LONG Area	III Corps Area.

Starting Point	Time.	Route	Remarks.
Junction of OUERVILLE - GAMACHES Road and LONGROY - GAMACHES Road.	1.0.p.m.	GAMACHES - MAINEIERRE - VISMES.	Column under command of Capt.E.H.TROKES, 66th Bde. A.E.F.
		HUPPY - PONT REMY Cross Rds.S.E. of BELLENCOURT - AILLY.	Supplies from R.S.O. HARTAINNEVILLE.
		BRUCAMP - VIGNACOURT - FLESSELLES - VILLERS BOCAGE	Not to enter FLESSELLES before 11.a.m. Supplies R.S.O. PONT REMY. Guide will meet Transport at Western entrance of VILLERS BOCAGE.

Appendix No. 6.

SECRET.   OPERATION ORDER No. 44   Copy No. 9
by
Lieut.Colonel J.H.PORTER, D.S.O.
Cmdg 2/6th North Staffordshire Regiment

Refce Sheets AMIENS 17)
            DIEPPE 18)
            ABBEVILLE 24) 1/100,000   dated 21st June 1918.
            LENS 11)

1. MOVE — The Training Cadre 2/6th North Staffs Regiment will move by bus route on June 21st from GAMACHES Area to III Corps Area.

2. STARTING POINT — Battalion Headquarters.

3. TIME — 7.a.m.

4. EMBUSSING — The Training Cadre will embus at 8.30.a.m. at the head of the column facing S.E. at Cross Roads just N. of & in Gas Works just N.W. of GAMACHES on Main Road.

5. BAGGAGE — Officers' Valises, Blankets and surplus stores will be handed in to Q.M.Stores by 5.30.a.m.

6. DRESS — Full Marching Order.

7. HEADQUARTERS — Battn. Headquarters will close at BAZINVAL at 7.a.m. and re-open at destination on arrival.

8. ACKNOWLEDGE.

(Sd) H.T.MORGAN,
Capt & Adjutant.
2/6th North Staffs Regiment.

Distribution -
Copy No. 1   198th Inf. Bde.
        2   C.O.
     3-6   Os.C.Companies
        7   Q.M.
        8   R.S.M.
        9   War Diary
      10   File.

Appendix 7.

SECRET.   OPERATION ORDER NO. 45   Copy No. 9
                              by
                  Lieut. Colonel J.H.PORTER, D.S.O.
                    Cmdg 2/6th North Staffs Regiment.

Reference Sheet AMIENS 17, 1/100,000.
                LENS 44, 1/100,000.   d/- 25/6/18.
----

1. MOVE.   -   The Training Cadre 2/6th North Staffs Regt. will
                        move by march route to-morrow, 26th June, to
                        PIERGOT, to be attached to the 1st Battn. ???
                        Infantry Regiment.

2. STARTING POINT   -   Battalion Headquarters.

3. TIME.   -   7.15.a.m.

4. COMMAND.   -   Capt. J.SWALES, M.C. will be in command, and will
                        conduct the column to the Church at PIERGOT,
                        where he will report to the Adjutant.

5. BAGGAGE   -   All Officers' Valises, Blankets rolled in bundles
                        of ten, tents, tent poles etc. will be stacked at
                        the Q.M. Stores at ?.a.m.
                        The Q.M. will arrange for the G.S.Wagon to return
                        and convey stores that are not able to be conveyed
                        on the first journey.

6. DRESS   -   Full Marching Order.

7.   ACKNOWLEDGE.

                            (sd) H.T.MORGAN,
                                     Capt & Adjutant.
                                     2/6th North Staffs Regiment.

    Distribution -
        Copy No. 1 186th Inf.Bde.
                 2 C.O.
                 3 - 6 O.C. Coys.
                 6 R.S.M.
                 7 Q.M.
                 8 War Diary
                 10 File.

Appendix No.8.

SECRET   OPERATION ORDER NO: 46:   COPY NO: 9
by
Lieut:Colonel J:H:PORTER D:S:O:
Cadg: 2/6th: North Staffordshire Regiment.

Refce: Sheet LENS 11, 1/100,000   d/ 26/6/18

1: MOVE: — The Training Cadre, 2/6th North Staffs: Regiment, will move by March route to-morrow, June 27th, to BERTEAUCOURT (O 8: 2:6:)

2: ROUTE: — PERNELOUT – VILLERS BOCAGE – FIENVILLERS – VIGNACOURT – BERTEAUCOURT:

3: STARTING POINT:- Battalion Headquarters:

4: TIME: — 8:a:m:

5: DRESS: — Full marching order:

6: BAGGAGE: — Officers' Valises (lightly packed for use on night 27/28th), Blankets (rolled in bundles of ten), mess stores and sufficient cooking utensils for night of 27/28th will be stacked at Q:M:Stores ready for loading on G:S:Wagon and Mess Cart at 7a:m:
All surplus stores to be carted on the lorry will be stacked separately at Q:M:Stores at 7:15a:m:

7: TRANSPORT: — Transport will be with Cadre: Additional Transport (1/3rd Lorry) is allotted to this Battn:Cadre:
The Q:M: will arrange for a guide to be at the 17th Manchesters Headquarters to guide lorry to this Headquarters:

8: SUPPLIES — The Q:M: will arrange for supplies for personnel proceeding by Lorry to be sent on Lorry:
Supplies for personnel proceeding by road will proceed on G:S:Wagon:

9: ADVANCE PARTY — Capt:J:Swales, M:C: will proceed ahead to BERTEAU-COURT in order to ascertain and arrange for accommodation:

10: ACKNOWLEDGE

(Sd) H:T:MORGAN:
Capt:&Adjutant:
2/6th North Staffs: Regiment:

Distribution:-
Copy No:1   198th Inf: Bde:
2   C:O:
3-6   O:C:Companies:
7   Q:M:
8   R:S:M:
9   War Diary:
10   File:

appendix No. 9.

SECRET.   OPERATION ORDER NO. 47   Copy No. 9
by
Lieut. Colonel J.H. PORTER, D.S.O.
Cmdg 2/6th North Staffordshire Regiment.

Refce LENS 11, 1/100,000
ABBEVILLE 44, 1/100,000   d/- 27/6/18.

----

1. MOVE.   – The Training Cadre, 2/6th North Staffordshire
                    Regiment will move by march route on June 28th
         YAUCOURT   to XXXXXXXXXXXXXXXXXXXXX in the LONG Area to be
                    attached to the 199th Infantry Brigade.

2. ROUTE   – MOUFLERS – AILLY LE HAUT CLOCHER.

3. STARTING POINT – East end of bridge over the River NIEUVRE.

4. TIME   – 8 a.m.

5. DRESS   – Full Marching Order less Packs. Haversacks will
                    be worn on the back.

6. BAGGAGE   – The G.S. Wagon will call at Officers' Billets
                    to collect Valises at 7 a.m. All Packs with
                    blankets attached will be stacked at the Q.M.
                    Stores by 7 a.m.

7. TRANSPORT   – The Transport will accompany the Battalion.

8. ACKNOWLEDGE.

                          (Sd) H.T. MORGAN,
                                Capt & Adjutant.
                                2/6th North Staffs Regiment.

    Distribution –
        Copy No. 1   199 Inf. Bde.
                  2   C.O.
                  3   O.C. "A" Company
                  4   O.C. "B" Company
                  5   O.C. "C" Company
                  6   O.C. "D" Company
                  7   Quartermaster.
                  8   R.S.M.
                  9   War Diary
                 10   File.

appendix 1.

SECRET: OPERATION ORDER NO: 48   COPY NO: 9
                        by
               Lieut: Colonel J:H:PORTER, D:S:O:
               Cmdg: 2/6th North Staffordshire Regiment:

Reference Maps 11, 1/100,000
          ABBEVILLE 14, 1/100,000   d/- 2/7/18

1: MOVE: The Training Cadre, 2/6th North Staffs: Regiment, will
                      move by march route on 3rd: July to BEARNAVILLE, and
                      will be administered by Composite Brigade (commanded
                      by Lieut: Colonel HANCOCK, 2/5th Manchester Regiment),
                      on arrival at DOULLENS:

2: ROUTE: BUSSUS BUSSUEL-MAISON-ROLLAND thence to main ABBEVILLE-
                      DOULLENS Road to BEARNAVILLE:

3: STARTING POINT: Battalion Headquarters:

4: TIME: 6:45 a:m:

5: BAGGAGE: All Officers' Valises, Blankets, Stores etc: will
                      be stacked at Q:M:Stores at 6 a:m:
                      One lorry will report at these Headquarters after
                      reporting at 18th: Kings Liverpool Regt: and 2/5th
                      Lincoln Regt: to collect baggage: This lorry is due
                      at 18th Kings Liverpool Regt: H:Qrs: at 8 a:m: and
                      will deposit baggage at DOULLENS:

6: ADVANCE & REAR   Capt: P:L:BURT will proceed to BEARNAVILLE to make
   PARTY: arrangements for billeting, and will report to
                      Town Major, BEARNAVILLE:
                      Capt: C:T:GARRISH will remain behind to hand over
                      to 17th: Manchester Regt: and will settle all
                      billeting claims:

7: DRESS: Full Marching Order:

8: TRAINING STORES: All small targets, documents and training stores
                      belonging to this area will be handed over to
                      incoming Unit:

9: HEADQUARTERS: Bn:H:Qrs: YAUCOURT will close at 6:45 a:m: and
                      re-open at BEARNAVILLE on arrival:

10: ACKNOWLEDGE:

                              (Sd) H:T:MORGAN,
                                      Capt & Adjutant:
                                      2/6th North Staffs Regiment:

          Distribution-
                    Copy No: 1   199 Inf: Bde:
                             2   O:C:
                           3-6- C:C:Companies
                             7   Q:M:
                             8   M:S:M:
                             9   War Diary:
                            10   File

Appendix 2

SECRET   OPERATION ORDER NO. 42   Copy No. 9
by
Lieut. Colonel J.H. PORTER, D.S.O.
Cmdg 2/6th North Staffordshire Regiment

Refce. Sheet LENS 11, 1/100,000   d/- 3/7/18.

1. MOVE.	The Training Cadre 2/6th North Staffs Regt. will move by march route tomorrow, 4th July, to DOULLENS, and on arrival will be administered by Composite Brigade (Commanded by Lieut. Colonel HANCOCK, 2/6th Manchester Regiment).
2. ROUTE.	FIENVILLERS - HARDINVAL - HEM - DOULLENS.
3. STARTING POINT	Battalion Headquarters.
4. TIME	6.45.a.m.
5. DRESS	Full Marching Order.
6. BAGGAGE.	All Officers' Valises, Blankets, Stores, etc. will be stacked at Q.M. Stores at 6.a.m.
7. SUPPLIES.	Rations for consumption on the 5th instant will be drawn from the Refilling Point at BEAUVAL.
8. HEADQUARTERS	Bn.H.Qrs. will close at BERNAVILLE at 6.45.a.m. and re-open at DOULLENS on arrival.
9. ACKNOWLEDGE.	

(Sd) H.T. MORGAN,
Capt & Adjutant.
2/6th North Staffs Regiment.

Distribution
     Copy No. 1 Brigade.
             2. C.O.
             3 -6 Os.C. Companies.
             7 Q.M.
             8 R.S.M.
             9 War Diary
            10 File.

SECRET.

Appendix 3.

OPERATION ORDER NO. 50

Copy No.....

by

Lieut.Colonel J.H.PORTER, D.S.O.
Cmdg 2/6th North Staffordshire Regiment.

Refce.Maps Sheet LENS 11, 1/100,000
DIEPPE 16, 1/100,000.
dated 21st July 1918.

---

1. **MOVE.** — The Training Cadre, 2/6th North Staffs Regiment will move by March and Train Route to the ABANCOURT - SERQUEX (L of C.) Area on July 22nd 1918.

2. **ROUTE.** — March Route from DOULLENS to CANDAS NORD STATION.

3. **ENTRAINING STN.** — CANDAS NORD STATION.

4. **DETRAINING STN.** — SERQUEX

5. **TIME.** — The personnel of the Training Cadre will parade at 1.p.m. to entrain at 4.p.m.

6. **BAGGAGE.** — All Officers' Baggage, Surplus Stores, Blankets, and Mess Property will be stacked outside the Q.M. Stores at 10.a.m.
A Lorry will be at the disposal of the Q.M. to convey Stores to Station at CANDAS. This Lorry will report at 10.a.m.

7. **DRESS.** — Full Marching Order. Steel Helmets will be carried beneath the Supporting Straps on the back of the Pack.

8. **TRANSPORT.** — The Transport, under Capt.R.Burton, will parade at 11.a.m. and proceed by March Route to CANDAS NORD STATION, where it will entrain and proceed with the remainder of the Training Cadre.

9. **ADVANCE PARTY** — An advance party, consisting of Capt.F.E.Burt, Lt. & Q.M. W.C.Johnson and C.Q.M.S.Crawford will report to the R.T.O. at CANDAS at 11.a.m., and proceed by train No.1 which leaves at 12 noon. They will be met at Station of Detrainment by a representative of 66the Division, who will give instructions as to Billets.

10. **SUPPLIES.** — The unexpired portion of the day's rations (22nd) will be carried by the man. Rations for the 23rd will be carried on the Baggage Wagon. Rations for the 24th will be issued at the Station of Entrainment. Rations for consumption on the 25th will be drawn on arrival in the new area by Unit from the nearest Supply Depot. O.C. Divisional Train will arrange and inform Units when and where to draw.

11. **ENTRAINING STATE** — Capt.R.Burton will be responsible for obtaining an Entraining State from this Office, and will hand it over to Officer supervising entraining at CANDAS, for transmission to the R.T.O.

12. **CLEANLINESS** — The Orderly Officer will be responsible for inspecting all billets, and handing them over in a clean condition to a representative of the Town Major.

13. **HEADQUARTERS** — H.Qrs. will close at DOULLENS at 1.p.m. and re-open at destination on arrival.

14. **ACKNOWLEDGE.**

(Sd) H.T.MORGAN,

Captn & Adjutant,
2/6th North Staffs Regt.

Distribution:-
```
Copy No. 1    Composite Brigade.
         2    Town Major DOULLENS
         3    Commanding Officer
         4    O.C. "A" Company
         5    O.C. "B" Company
         6    O.C. "C" Company
         7    O.C. "D" Company
         8    Quartermaster
         9    R.S.M.
        10    War Diary
        11    File.
```

Appendix 3.

SECRET. OPERATION ORDER NO. 50 Copy No.....
by
Lieut.Colonel J.H.PORTER, D.S.O.
Cmdg 2/6th North Staffordshire Regiment.

Refce. Maps Sheet LENS 11, 1/100,000
DIEPPE 16, 1/100,000.   dated 21st July 1918.

---

1. **MOVE.** — The Training Cadre, 2/6th North Staffs Regiment will move by March and Train Route to the ABANCOURT - SERQUEX (L of C.) Area on July 22nd 1918.

2. **ROUTE.** — March Route from DOULLENS to CANDAS NORD STATION.

3. **ENTRAINING STN.** — CANDAS NORD STATION.

4. **DETRAINING STN.** — SERQUEX

5. **TIME.** — The personnel of the Training Cadre will parade at 1.p.m. to entrain at 4.p.m.

6. **BAGGAGE.** — All Officers' Baggage, Surplus Stores, Blankets, and Mess Property will be stacked outside the Q.M. Stores at 10.a.m.
A Lorry will be at the disposal of the Q.M. to convey Stores to Station at CANDAS. This Lorry will report at 10.a.m.

7. **DRESS.** — Full Marching Order. Steel Helmets will be carried beneath the Supporting Straps on the back of the pack.

8. **TRANSPORT.** — The Transport, under Capt.R.Burton, will parade at 11.a.m. and proceed by March Route to CANDAS NORD STATION, where it will entrain and proceed with the remainder of the Training Cadre.

9. **ADVANCE PARTY** — An advance party, consisting of Capt.F.E.Burt, Lt. & Q.M. W.C.Johnson and C.Q.M.S.Crawford will report to the R.T.O. at CANDAS at 11.a.m., and proceed by train No.1 which leaves at 12 noon. They will be met at Station of Detrainment by a representative of 66the Division, who will give instructions as to Billets.

10. **SUPPLIES.** — The unexpired portion of the day's rations (22nd) will be carried by the man. Rations for the 23rd will be carried on the Baggage Wagon. Rations for the 24th will be issued at the Station of Entrainment. Rations for consumption on the 25th will be drawn on arrival in the new area by Unit from the nearest Supply Depot. O.C. Divisional Train will arrange and inform Units when and where to draw.

11. **ENTRAINING STATE** — Capt.R.Burton will be responsible for obtaining an Entraining State from this Office, and will hand it over to Officer supervising entraining at CANDAS, for transmission to the R.T.O.

12. **CLEANLINESS** — The Orderly Officer will be responsible for inspecting all billets, and handing them over in a clean condition to a representative of the Town Major.

13. **HEADQUARTERS** — H.Qrs. will close at DOULLENS at 1.p.m. and re-open at destination on arrival.

14. **ACKNOWLEDGE.**

(Sd) H.T.MORGAN,
Captn & Adjutant,
2/6th North Staffs Regt.

Distribution:-

Copy No.	1	Composite Brigade.
	2	Town Major DOULLENS
	3	Commanding Officer
	4	O.C. "A" Company
	5	O.C. "B" Company
	6	O.C. "C" Company
	7	O.C. "D" Company
	8	Quartermaster
	9	R.S.M.
	10	War Diary
	11	File.

SECRET   OPERATION ORDER NO.50   Copy No....10.
                                by
                     Lieut.Colonel J.H.PORTER, D.S.O.
                     Cmdg 2/6th North Staffordshire Regiment.
                     - - - -
                                                    d/- 30/7/18.

1. MOVE.   The W.Os. N.C.Os. and Privates of the Training Cadre
                    2/6th North Staffs Regiment, with the exception of
                    Officers' Servants as detailed, will proceed to
                    join the 46th Division to-morrow, 31st July.

2. ROUTE.   March Route to ROMESCAMPS Station; by train from
                    there to Railhead, 46th Division.

3. STARTING POINT   Battalion Headquarters.

4. TIME   7.45.a.m. to entrain at 10.30.a.m.

5. DRESS   Full Marching Order. Steel Helmets will be carried
                    under the Supporting Straps on the back of the pack.

6. RATIONS.   Unconsumed portion of the days rations will be
                    carried and rations for the 1st August will be
                    taken in Bulk.

7. BAGGAGE.   All blankets will be rolled in bundles of ten and
                    stacked at Q.M.Stores at 7.a.m. The Q.M. will
                    arrange to hand these over, together with any other
                    Regtl. equipment, to Q.M.S. 198th Inf.Bde. who will
                    report at this Camp for that purpose.

8. COMMAND.   Capt.F.E.BURT will act as draft conducting Officer
                    and will hand over draft to 4/6th North Staffs Regt
                    He will obtain all documents from Bn.O.R. before
                    leaving and will obtain a receipt for them from
                    4/6th North Staffs Regiment. He will return to
                    this location on completion of duty.

9. TRANSPORT.   1st Line Transport with the exception of Rides will
                    accompany the draft to the entraining station, where
                    it will be taken over complete, together with the
                    drivers of the Water Cart and Mess Cart, by the 66th
                    Divl. Train. The Rides will be handed over to
                    543 Coy.A.S.C. and the Q.M. will obtain receipts for
                    all Transport handed over.

10.ARMOURERS.   Armourer Staff Sergeant will not accompany Battn.
                    Training Cadre. He will report to D.A.D.O.S. 66th
                    Division to-morrow.

11. ACKNOWLEDGE.

                            (Sd) H.T.MORGAN,   Captain & Adjutant.
                                                 2/6th North Staffs Regiment.

        Distribution - Copy No.1   198th Inf.Bde.
                             2   C.O.
                          3 - 6   O.C. Companies.
                             7   Q.M.
                             8   R.S.M.
                             9   Capt.BURT.
                            10   War Diary.
                            11   File.

ROUTINE ORDERS
by
Lieut.Col.J.H.PORTER, D.S.O.
Cmdg 2/6th North Staffordshire Regiment.

%/- 30/7/18.

(a). DUTIES.   Orderly Officer for to-morrow..Capt.R.BURTON.

(b) VALETE.   It is regreted that it has been found necessary to disband this Battalion. The Commanding Officer regrets very much that it should have been found necessary for this step to be taken, but wishes to assure all ranks that it reflects no discredit on the Battn., but is purely due to the exigencies of the service.
    Before the Battn. is disbanded the Commanding Officer wishes to thank all Officers, Warrant Officers, Non-Commissioned Officers and men of the Training Cadre for the splendid way in which they have always supported him, both before the Battalion was reduced to a Training Cadre and whilst the Training Cadre has been in existence, and assures them that the work which they have done has been very much appreciated.
    Most of the personnel are proceeding to join the 1/6th Battn. North Staffordshire Regiment, and he feels sure that when they are amongst their own friends they will not forget, and always uphold, the excellent name which the 2/6th North Staffordshire Regiment has always held, and that they will do all in their power to maintain the high traditions and fair name of the North Staffordshire Regiment.
    The Commanding Officer wishes all "GOD SPEED" and "GOOD LUCK"

(Sd) H.T.MORGAN,
Capt & Adjutant,
2/6th North Staffs Reg.

www.ingramcontent.com/pod-product-compliance
Lightning Source LLC
Chambersburg PA
CBHW081430160426
43193CB00013B/2242